DATE DUE

NOV.05.1996			
FEB.21.1997			
GAYLORD			PRINTED IN U.S.A.

INNOVATION AND CHANGE
IN THE HUMAN SERVICES

INNOVATION AND CHANGE IN THE HUMAN SERVICES

By

NICHOLAS D. RICHIE, MSW, PH.D.

Associate Professor
Health Administration Department
Florida Atlantic University

and

DIANE E. ALPERIN, MS, ACSW, LCSW

Associate Professor
Social Work Department
Florida Atlantic University

CHARLES C THOMAS • PUBLISHER
Springfield • Illinois • U.S.A.

Published and Distributed Throughout the World by

CHARLES C THOMAS · PUBLISHER
2600 South First Street
Springfield, Illinois 62794-9265

© *1992 by* CHARLES C THOMAS · PUBLISHER
ISBN 0-398-05763-x
Library of Congress Catalog Card Number: 91-30178

Printed in the United States of America
SC-R-3

Library of Congress Cataloging-in-Publication Data

Richie, Nicholas D.
    Innovation and change in the human services / by Nicholas D.
Richie and Diane E. Alperin.
        p.   cm.
    Includes bibliographical references and indexes.
    ISBN 0-398-05763-X
    1. Human services—United States—History—20 century.
I. Alperin, Diane E.   II. Title.
HV91.R53   1991
361.973′09′04—dc20   91-30178
                                                                          CIP

This book is dedicated to our families, our teachers, our colleagues and our students.

CONTENTS

LIST OF TABLES

LIST OF FIGURES

INNOVATION AND CHANGE
IN THE HUMAN SERVICES

PART I

THE EVOLUTION OF HUMAN SERVICES
IN THE TWENTIETH CENTURY

INTRODUCTION

Human services have been defined as those disciplines which under-
take to help people solve their problems of living and growing
(Epstein, 1981). Examples include the activities of health professionals,
social workers, and criminal justice workers—in such fields as child
welfare, crime and delinquency, disability and physical handicap, health
care, family counseling, housing, income maintenance, labor relations,
mental health, migration and resettlement, nursing home care, protective services, and recreational services, among others (Minahan, 1987).

Various human services organizations (hereafter, HSOs) have evolved
to offer such services, and have as their primary function "to define or
alter a person's behavior, attributes, and social status in order to maintain
or enhance his well-being" (Hasenfeld and English, 1974, p. 6). Over
the course of the Twentieth Century, the overall provision of human
services has evolved in an incremental, nonsystematic manner, and this
evolution has varied somewhat, depending upon purpose, sponsorship,
external and internal factors—among others.

HSOs may be divided into three main categories:

1. Governmental
2. Voluntary
3. Private

We shall here use these three terms in the same way as Kahn, recognizing that the terms are variously defined by writers in the human services
field. By governmental, we mean services that are a unit of government
at any level (Federal, state, county, municipal). By voluntary, we refer to
agencies which are not-for-profit, community-based. By private, we refer
to for-profit agencies—also known as investor-owned, tax-paying (Kahn,
1984).

Each of these types will be discussed below, but overall, the twentieth

3

century has seen a continued increase in demand for human services by the public. The voluntary sector, in particular, has been limited in its ability to meet these increased demands due to the pervasiveness of some of these needs, the cost to ameliorate them, historical and social conditions, and demographic shifts (Jimenez, 1990).

A major criticism of much of the human services sector today is the lack of comprehensive, coordinated coverage of the problems impacting individuals, families, and communities. Indeed, even the identification of which problems are worthy of focus is debatable (Morris, 1986).

Using the sociological theory of functionalism, one tends to view the social world in systemic terms, with an emphasis on equilibrium/ homeostasis, in which interrelated parts interact to accomplish mutually-desired goals (Turner, 1982; Chambliss, 1973; Stoesz, 1988). As the following descriptions of the three main types of HSOs indicate, a holistic, coordinated approach in the human services will require considerable effort to achieve, but the authors do not consider the task impossible, and will make a specific proposal in Part III of this volume.

GOVERNMENTAL HSOS

At the turn of the Twentieth Century, the United States—which had inherited the "Poor Law" tradition of Elizabethan England (Kohlert, 1989)—had endured more than one hundred years of promoting the ideal of laissez-faire, free-enterprise capitalism. When combined with the rugged individualism espoused on the Western frontier, there was little incentive at the federal level to voluntarily assume national responsibility for many of the services currently believed to be the responsibility of government (Lee and Benjamin, 1988). It is true that at the dawn of the Republic, the federal government established the Marine Hospital Fund for the Relief of Sick and Disabled Seamen, in 1798—to protect merchant marines in a society highly dependent upon sea-trade for its economic well-being (Mullan, 1989). It is also true that in the nineteenth century, universal public education was made available by the individual states (Gutek, 1970). However, Dorothea Dix's struggle to establish mental hospital systems within the respective states, while ultimately successful, illustrates the reluctance of government at various levels, to become involved in the direct provision of human services (Lee and Benjamin, 1988).

As Wilensky and Lebeaux have argued, with increasing industrialization in the Twentieth Century, have come greater (and new) social problems which require a concerted, broad-based governmental approach (Wilensky and Lebeaux, 1958). Thus, at the turn of the century, fear of epidemics of contagious diseases, particularly in crowded urban environments, prompted the provision of public health services—at the municipal, county, state, or federal level, depending on the nature and severity of the problem. Popular techniques at that time were mass immunizations and quarantine (Rosen, 1958).

At the same time, widespread reports of danger to the public's health (such as in the case of spoiled meat, milk, other foodstuffs and questionable medications and medical devices) prompted the federal government to establish the Biologics Control Act in 1902, which gave the Hygenic Laboratory (later to evolve into the National Institutes of Health) regulatory authority in the production and sale of antitoxins and vaccines (Mullan, 1989). The Food and Drug Administration followed soon, in 1906 (Luce, 1988, p. 290). Related governmental agencies were established at the state and/or local levels, in many instances.

Another problem, related to the proliferation of injury and death in the workplace as industrialization increased, led to the passage of Worker's Compensation Laws, in the various states, beginning in 1911 (Mowbray and Blanchard, 1955). Industrialization also contributed to the social problems of overcrowding, unemployment, and poverty, which were the impetus for states to become active in the welfare role. "Mothers' aid" and "mothers' pension" programs evolved to assist children in fatherless families. Some states followed with programs that focused on specific populations, such as the blind and disabled (DiNitto and Dye, 1987, p. 25).

World War I, with its massive mobilization of men to be examined for service, and possibly accepted for military duty, led to a large-scale natural experiment, in which authorities were able to collect a great deal of data, within a relatively short period of time, on the male population. Results of the analysis indicated widespread illiteracy and undereducation, malnutrition, untreated chronic and acute problems, and poor dental care (Engleman and Joy, 1975). When resources were freed-up again, after the War, there was both professional and public pressure for programs at various levels of government which could deal with such problems. In addition, the long-term rehabilitation of World War I veterans, who had been gassed or otherwise disabled, required new solutions—sometimes including the development of "new professions"—

particularly those involving vocational and psychological counseling, occupational and physical therapy (Stanfield, 1990).

Still, despite these developments at various levels in the governmental sector during the first three decades of the twentieth century, it wasn't until the New Deal of the administration of President Franklin Roosevelt that a national approach to social welfare, as an important part of the broader human services spectrum, was initiated. The massive collapse of the economy at the time of the Great Depression called for an equally massive approach to provide economic security to all (Miringoff, 1980). The landmark federal legislation, upon which so many other federal human services programs have been built, is, of course, the Social Security Act of 1935 (Social Security Act of 1935, 42 U.S. Code, Section 301). Originally meant to provide a financial retirement "cushion" in old age, the Act has been repeatedly amended to include provision of such human services as Maternal and Child Health Care Grants (Title V), Medicare (Title XVIII) and Medicaid (Title XIX), among others (Feingold, 1966; Shonick, 1988). Since that time, government at all levels—municipal, county, state, and federal—has increasingly become involved in the provision of human services, often through shared programs.

Stern believes that the expansion of governmental involvement in the human services at the time of the New Deal was due to the presence of two critical coalitions: (1) an *electoral* coalition—which provided long-term general support for the growth of the federal government's role in the human services; and (2) a coalition *within* government—composed of administrators, legislators, and lobbyists at the federal level. This group took advantage of the stable electoral situation, and used it to expand such involvements by the federal government (Stern, 1984).

One attempt by the federal government, since the early post-World War II years, to achieve more rational, systematic human services—at least in the health care area, has been the proliferation of legislation related to health planning (Richie, 1978). The Hospital Survey and Construction Act—also known as Hill-Burton (Public Law 79–725, 1946)—provided federal aid for construction of voluntary hospitals in rural areas in states which had Health Planning Councils capable of assessing need. The Law was later amended in 1954 to include funding for modernization or replacement of hospitals in urban areas (Hyman, 1976).

The next major step in health planning occurred in October 1965, with the passage of the Heart Disease, Cancer and Stroke Amendments of 1965 (Public Law 89–239, 1965)—which led to the establishment of Regional Medical Programs. The latter were cooperative arrangements in fifty-six health regions, through which existing hospitals, research and medical centers were organized and charged with evaluating overall health needs within each region. Amendments added in 1970 expanded the scope beyond heart disease, stroke, and cancer (Hyman, 1976).

Reports of various commissions over the years, addressing the issue of health planning, culminated in a philosophy of regional *comprehensive* planning, which became law with the passage of the Comprehensive Health Planning and Public Health Service Amendments of 1966 (Public Law 89–749, 1966). This legislation authorized funds for state and areawide comprehensive health planning agencies. By 1974, there were 218 Comprehensive Health Planning Agencies, covering about 79 percent of the U.S. population. These agencies were criticized on a number of grounds, including their having small, underpaid staffs, their being controlled by local health care providers who donated some of the matching funds, having insufficient representation of consumers on the advisory councils, and lack of guidance from Washington (U.S. Department of Health, Education and Welfare, 1976, pp. 97–104).

A major effort to combine the best intentions of the above-mentioned federal health planning legislation was attempted by the passage of the National Health Planning and Resources Development Act of 1974 (Public Law 93–641, 93rd Congress). The Act was passed in order to: (1) strengthen Comprehensive Health Planning efforts—largely through mandatory development of certificate-of-need review processes; and (2) to combine in one program the earlier Hill-Burton, Regional Medical Programs and Comprehensive Health Planning legislation—in order to reduce duplication of effort and confusion among competing/overlapping regulatory entities.

It should be pointed out that various efforts in the area of *mental health* planning were occurring simultaneously, after World War II. As indicated earlier, since the 19th century, state governments had assumed responsibility for treating mental illness (through their respective state-wide networks of psychiatric hospitals). However, federal interest in the problem of planning for mental health was first expressed in the National Mental Health Act of 1946 (Public Law 79–487, 1946)—which specifically provided for the inclusion of mental health problems in the grant-in-aid programs of the Public Health Service, and also established the National Institute of Mental Health. Subsequent legislation has included the authorization of grants to facilitate research into resources and methods for care of the mentally ill, special project grants particularly aimed at the problems of state mental hospitals, legislation addressed to the problem of mental retardation, construction and initial staffing of community mental health centers, treatment and rehabilitation facilities for alcoholics and narcotic addicts, and drug education programs (Wilson and Neuhauser, 1976).

Riley underscores the point that the federal government's involvement in the human services has not only been gradual, but often indirect — that is, in the form of reimbursement to states which directly provide the services. He sees Title XX of the Social Security Act Amendments, which became effective in 1975, as a milestone in such federal involvement, in that it provided reimbursement to states for a variety of services, such as: day care; child/adult protective services; counseling; service to the elderly; foster/group home care; and homemaker/chore services. States provide some of these services directly, but may also purchase them from voluntary agencies. To the extent possible, governmental monitoring and evaluation is expected to take place (Riley, 1981). One advantage to the government, of contracting with voluntary agencies, is the elimination of the need to set up governmental programs at considerable capital expense (Rice, 1990).

Making the above-mentioned evolution of governmental involvement in human services difficult has been the fact that the United States is a pluralistic society, which today has a mixed economy, with both capitalistic and socialistic elements (Friedman, 1963). Both approaches reflect widely differing political premises. On the one extreme is the free-enterprise model, mentioned earlier, which would keep government involvement in the daily lives and problems of its citizens to a minimum. Those holding this view tend to see many of the human services currently being offered by the government, or advocated for governmental sponsorship, as "privileges," not "rights." At the other extreme, those who see the provision of human services to all as the total responsibility of government at one level or another, view them as "rights," rather than "privileges." And in between, are many who hold mixed views — depending on the problem at hand, the target population, the strength of government revenues, and a host of other variables (Donabedian, 1973, pp. 1–15).

A major upshot of the pluralism present in American society is the appearance of "cycles" of expansion and contraction, dependent upon whether compassion or pragmatism dominate the psyche of the citizenry and their legislators/policy-makers (Miringoff, 1980). Thus, the 1930s and 1960s may be seen as periods of expansion, while the 1950s, 1970s, and 1980s may be seen as periods of contraction (Jimenez, 1990).

Morris attributes this cyclical activity partially to the fact that, unlike modern Europe, the U.S. has only occasionally had periods where there has been a widely-accepted consensus to assure the well-being of all citizens through governmental action. He points out that many of the recipients of "assistance" from governmental programs do not see (or choose not to see) that they are, in fact, receiving governmental aid. Thus, those who are most highly visible in the public eye tend to be participating in means-tested programs—dependent children, the blind, the disabled. Those receiving "earned" benefits (unemployment insurance, worker's compensation, veterans' benefits) usually do not equate themselves with the recipients of means-tested services. And rarely, if ever, do those who receive governmental benefits through the variety of complicated tax breaks available view themselves as recipients of governmental largesse (Morris, 1986).

The authors of a recent monograph argue that the view of our country's welfare system as a mess and jumble of undesirable, unaffordable programs is incorrect, and unfair. They argue that most welfare spending goes either to elderly recipients of social security or to people who are not expected to work (such as the disabled)—and that both these programs have long been supported by the American people. When Medicare, Medicaid, and Social Security are viewed as helping to keep millions out of poverty, rather than as an attempt to end poverty entirely, the system should be credited with more success than it usually receives in times of high-profile rhetoric (Marmor et al., 1990).

The evolution of governmental HSOs in the Twentieth Century may thus be summarized as follows:

Pre-1900: Governmental involvement was kept to a minimum in conjunction with the American "ideal" of laissez-faire, free-enterprise capitalism. Religious/charitable organizations provided most of the available human services—but often in a nonsystematic manner, for narrowly-defined target populations. When governmental involvement occurred, in contradiction to espoused American ideals, it was usually precipitated by overriding national economic concerns (fear of epidemics which might destroy the economy through a loss of productivity, fear of an illiterate, nonproductive population—in the absence of universal education, etc.). In this period, governmental involvement in the human services was largely reactive, and in response to external and internal threats to the economy, although there were some limited proactive attempts by local governments to pay for private care under contract — discussed below (Friedlander, 1961).

1900-1930:   Governmental involvement in HSOs, although limited, partially grew during this period in reaction to the "muckrakers"—writers who exposed corruption by government officials, and industrialists involved in monopolies and cartels, precipitating action to protect citizens from unsafe products/situations. An increase in industrial accidents/ deaths, prompted state governments to enact workers' compensation laws, and fear of large-scale epidemics of communicable diseases prompted the expansion of public health activities. When the federal government assumed responsibility for the disabled veterans of World War I, services for this particular population were expanded.

In 1927, a blue-ribbon panel was established (which met until 1932) to discuss the role of government in health care. Its Final Report, which became a landmark document, urged the establishment of government grants for the care of the indigent—as well as other "innovations," such as group practice by physicians and expansion of voluntary health insurance (Committee on the Costs of Medical Care, 1932).

1930-1970:   The Great Depression of the 1930s was a sufficient dispenser of human misery to precipitate the New Deal of President Franklin Roosevelt and the landmark Social Security Act of 1935. This federal law, and its amendments, increased the federal role in the provision of human services to a level not previously seen, and still crucial as the twentieth century nears its close. The 1940s brought World War II, and the necessity to concentrate on the war effort. However, after the War, funds were made available to deal with the multiple problems of returning veterans, and to expand the activities of the National Institutes of Health— particularly as regards heart disease, stroke, and cancer (concerns of the largely white, male, aging Congress of that period). A renewed focus on mental health was also a direct result of the War, with a need to attend to the mental illnesses of both soldiers and veterans. In 1946, the National Institute of Mental Health was established, in an effort to promote research into mental illness (Jansson, 1984, p. 441).

At this time, the long series of health planning legislation/amendments (discussed above) was initiated also. The Eisenhower Era of the 1950s, with its reemphasis on free enterprise during the cold war military build-up, slowed the acceleration of governmental involvement in the human services begun under Franklin Roosevelt. However, the creation, under Eisenhower, of the cabinet level Department of Health, Education and Welfare, in 1953, raised federal involvement in these areas to a level of greater visibility (Fenno, 1959; Lee, 1972). Over time, the gaps in services to the disadvantaged were so widely viewed as acute, that by the 1960s, President Lyndon Johnson's vision of a "Great Society" ushered in a "War on Poverty"—with a series of legislation designed to ameliorate the social problems of ethnic and racial minorities, and the elderly, in particular. Many of the resultant programs, based on a community-advocacy model, were short-lived, but the long-run effect was to heighten expectations about the federal role in the development of human services (Jimenez, 1990). The Head Start program, for preschoolers, the food stamp program, and an extensive body of research on poverty, are several remaining tangible legacies of the War on Poverty (Stern, 1984).

1970-Present: In the past several decades, inflation—fueled partly by the Vietnam War, contributed to a view of government as the "enemy," and a popular belief that there was too much government in peoples' lives. Campaigning on this note, Ronald Reagan won two landslide presidential elections and instituted eight years of substantial reductions in federal spending and a laissez-faire domestic policy (Glazer, 1984). The predominant ideology espoused that there was too much governmental interference in family life, resulting in an abrogation of individual liberty. The perceived failings of liberal administrations, such as the Johnson and Carter presidencies, were also used to reduce, or limit, federal involvement in the provision of human services (Jimenez, 1990). George Bush campaigned in 1988 on a "no new taxes" platform, with the implication of reduced social spending, despite real and projected future needs of an increasingly elderly population, the spread of AIDS, the need to retool rust belt industries, and other late twentieth-century problems. Leon Ginsberg expects the future of social and human services under the Bush Administration to be similar to the experience of the Reagan years (Ginsberg, 1989).

VOLUNTARY HSOS

At the turn of the twentieth century, the United States already had a considerable history, dating back to the earliest years of colonization of North America, of providing assistance on a voluntary, not-for-profit basis, to some of those in need. These activities were often originally embedded in a religious context, and related to beliefs of personal salvation. Secular organizations later developed, such as the Charity Organization Society (COS), which provided assistance (usually through aid-in-kind and home visits) to those with demonstrated financial need — particularly disadvantaged natives and recent immigrants. The COS incorporated values of the Protestant Ethic, encouraging the changing of personal habits and adoption of positive attitudes toward hard work (Jimenez, 1990; Johnson, 1986). According to Riley, the COS movement also promoted the idea that scientific methods could be used to cure the "illness" of poverty. One result of this view was the appearance of Mary Richmond's landmark book, on friendly visiting, which became a basic text for both professionals and volunteers (Riley, 1981; Richmond, 1899).

During the first several decades of the twentieth century, extensive changes occurred in American life. A "flood" of new immigrants took place at that time, whose needs overwhelmed many of the COS-derived voluntary agencies — at a point in history when governmental involvement was not very prominent in the human services. As a result, many of the immigrant groups formed "mutual-aid societies" to assist their constituents in getting settled in American society and surviving the adjustment (Briggs, 1978; Schiro, 1975).

Another example of voluntary, not-for-profit activity was the development of the charitable/philanthropic "foundation" — such as the Carnegie Foundation. The latter sponsored a study of medical education in the U.S. and Canada, which found the quality of physician training to be generally below acceptable standards. Released in 1910 and known as the "Flexner Report," the study recommended a modern medical education curriculum that included courses in the basic sciences, as well as supervised clinical experience, and an emphasis upon research. Many medical schools were closed down shortly thereafter — in large part due to the Flexner Report (Flexner, 1910).

The stresses of World War I and rapid industrialization were added to the pressures already impacting the millions of new immigrants — as well as those moving from rural to urban settings, and a body of social science knowledge slowly evolved, which placed greater emphasis on the *social environment* as a critical factor in influencing human behavior than had previously been the case.

The closest thing to a holistic approach to human services in those early years was the "settlement house," which encouraged the movement of middle-class intellectuals into depressed urban areas to provide a wide range of services to nearby residents. At the same time, individuals engaged in the settlement house movement supported legislation in such areas as limiting child labor, improving working conditions in general, separating juvenile offenders from adults, etc. (Addams, 1960; Jimenez, 1990; Martin, 1990). While the earlier focus had been largely upon relief and poverty, the pioneering work of individuals such as Mary Richmond broadened the scope of diagnosis and treatment for social problems (Richmond, 1917).

In 1930, on the voluntary level, the Family Welfare Association of America (later, Family Service Association of America—and currently, Family Service America) became the heir to the old COS, and the great philanthropic movement that took place in the U.S. after the Civil War (Rice, 1990). Such agencies emphasize a concern for families in their mission statement, and have roots in the Relief and Aid Societies of the early 1800s. The latter were organized in various communities by affluent volunteers who distributed relief, usually in-kind, via home visits. Their services, however, tended to be sporadic—often associated with "economic panics," which periodically swept across the nation. The needs these agencies attempted to meet were considerable, because of the limited responsibility taken by the government at that time, and the fact that there were no organized programs in the private sector (Minahan, 1987, p. 589). With the Social Security Act of 1935 providing some financial support for part of the population, and with the influx of Freudian, and other, psychological theories, a de-emphasis on the impact of the social environment emerged (Jimenez, 1990).

Riley has argued that the clientele of family service agencies has changed over the years, as the agencies themselves have evolved. In the early years, the poorest people in the population were served. Later, agency service was expanded to all income groups, after family service was perceived as entailing more than "charity". Since the mid-1960s, and the provision of a variety of governmental "anti-poverty" programs to accommodate the disadvantaged, family service programs have come to be viewed by some as mainly for the middle class, and therefore "irrelevant to the poor" (Riley, 1981). Blumenstein recommends a balancing of priorities, so that services are available for the poor, and yet the family service agencies can still remain financially viable, by carrying a sufficient caseload of nonpoor clients (Blumenstein, 1988).

Voluntary agencies continued to grow during the 1930s, helped in part by the passage of a Federal law in 1935, allowing corporate deductions for charitable donations—which gave a financial boost to many of these agencies (Leiby, 1978). After World War II, economic growth and an increase in the birth rate fueled the demand for service. Voluntary organizations joined community-wide fund-raising campaigns such as the Community Chest, Red Feather, and United Way. Clients served, however, tended to be predominantly middle-class, as agencies needed to appeal to larger corporate donors and their concerns (Jimenez, 1990).

Additional pressure from funding sources occurred when the federal government became highly involved with voluntary agencies during the Great Society of the Johnson Administration. Some agencies questioned whether they could maintain their professional integrity while receiving such funds—without becoming instead the "servants" of the federal government. Thus, during this period, many agencies placed arbitrary limits on the portion of government funds they would include in their budgets (Rice, 1990).

Traunstein distinguishes between two main types of voluntary, not-for-profit human services agencies which dominated the scene in twentieth century America: the community-based HSO and the mutual-aid/self-help agency (Traunstein, 1984). The community-based HSO is typified by the vast number of voluntary, community, not-for-profit hospitals which predominate in the United States. These HSOs were usually founded by public-minded citizens, who filed incorporation documents, and served as the first board members, in an attempt to provide the community as a whole with general hospital care (Perrow, 1965). In the COS agencies previously discussed, the boards were similarly populated, and only gradually added professional "secretaries" and service personnel. Community professionals, businessmen and unemployed, well-to-do women, who could give considerable time, populated the boards. As the workload increased, it was necessary to hire paid personnel. At the present time, the complexity of agency operations has resulted in a "new wave" of board members who expect a strong management to handle the day-to-day operations of the agency. One area where staff, management, and board members can contribute appropriately, is in the area of strategic long-range planning, which became popular in the 1980s (Rice, 1990).

On the other hand, according to Traunstein, mutual-aid/self-help HSOs have the following characteristics: (1) a majority of the general membership and Board share a condition stigmatized by society;

(2) greater than 50 percent of the members of the board or their relatives directly benefit from the agency's program; and (3) in the initial stages of agency life, the professional contribution at all organizational levels is minimal or nonexistent. Common examples are the host of self-help organizations started by parents of children born with rare or severely dysfunctional conditions. In the early stages, such agencies offer services that either are not being offered elsewhere, or which they perceive to be ineffective when provided by others (Traunstein, 1984).

While not within a structured agency framework, a discussion of the self-help movement in this century cannot neglect the contribution of Alcoholics Anonymous (AA). Starting in 1935 in Akron, Ohio, the AA concept has experienced tremendous growth and expansion and is available in 114 countries worldwide (Alcoholic Anonymous World Services, 1984, p. 18). It differs from the mutual-aid/self-help HSOs discussed by Traunstein in that *all* members share a stigmatized condition and *all* the members directly benefit from the agency's services, following a behaviorally-focused 12-step program. And while professionals are not directly involved in the delivery of self-help services, much attention has focused on the importance of professional understanding of this important resource (Gartner and Reissman, 1984; Pancoast, et al., 1983; Silverman, 1978; Willen, 1984).

Alcoholics Anonymous is just an example of one self-help group focusing on a habit disturbance. Powell offers a typology of self-help organizations which includes habit disturbances (such as AA), general purpose organizations (such as Emotions Anonymous), lifestyle organizations (such as Parents Without Partners), significant-other organizations (such as Al-Anon), and physical handicap organizations—such as Emphysema Anonymous (Powell 1987). The phenomenal growth of all these organizations in the last two decades is in part correlated with the trend toward client empowerment occurring in this same time-frame (Riessman, 1987).

Since the early 1970s, voluntary agencies have had to contend with increased demand for services, fluctuating governmental support in the form of grants, limited philanthropic support, and competition from the private, for-profit sector (to be discussed below). A recent nationwide survey of Family Service America agencies, reemphasizes the 1980s as a period of tremendous growth in need for services. At the same time, governmental funding and United Way funding did not experience growth, as these agencies relied more on revenue-producing sources for support (Alperin, unpublished manuscript, 1991). Wenocur and Reisch have published a particularly readable account of the problems these human services agencies have faced in a market economy (Wenocur and Reisch, 1989).

One of the most interesting developments in the 1970s was the proliferation of the not-for-profit "health maintenance organization" (HMO) concept (Gumbiner, 1975; Anderson, 1985). While there had been several well-known earlier attempts to combine comprehensive medical care with a prepaid premium (Donabedian, 1965; Ellwood, 1970), it wasn't until the federal government passed the Health Maintenance Organization Act of 1973 (Public Law 93–222, Section 1301, PHS Act)—which provided financial incentives for the development of such facilities, that HMOs received widespread attention. Initial growth was slow, but by the 1980s the idea seemed to take hold, in part because of the continuing rise in the cost of health care (Raffel and Raffel, 1989). One study that compared elderly HMO enrollees with another group receiving private care found that the former group was more satisfied with the cost of their health care. On the other hand, satisfaction with the doctor-patient relationship and convenience of care was higher in the latter group (Stein et al., 1989). In many communities today, consumers may have a choice among *several* HMOs, because of their prevalence (Berki et al., 1977).

Sidney Garfield published a classic article (Garfield, 1970) which attempted to illustrate that HMOs were capable of taking a holistic view, which, coupled with an insurance-based payment mechanism, allows the client to enter the system *before* acute illness occurs—for preventive purposes. This approach also allows client-provider interaction in the early stages of sickness, in order to prevent increased severity or disability often associated with untreated symptoms. An adaption of Garfield's model, based on his longtime experience with the Kaiser-Permanente Plan, is shown in Figure 1. As can be seen, at the entry point, in keeping with an emphasis on prevention (health maintenance), "well" and "worried well" clients have as much access to the system as the "sick" or "early sick." Specific services available include testing and referral (A), an acute sick care center (B), a health care center offering outpatient follow-up (C), and preventive maintenance services (D)—such as exercise programs, nutrition education, etc. Communication channels (depicted by arrows) are clearly defined and computer technology contributes to the storage, processing, and retrieval of client data.

FIGURE 1 A HEALTH MAINTENANCE ORGANIZATION (HMO) MODEL

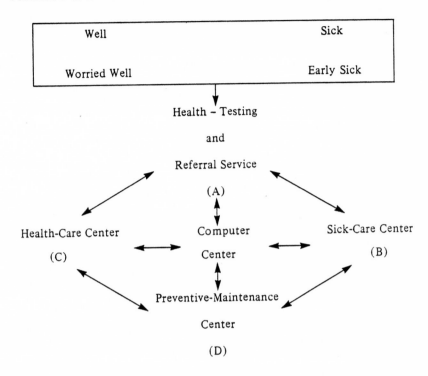

Adapted from Sidney Garfield, "The Delivery of Medical Care" *Scientific American*, *222*(4): 15–23, 1970.

In more recent years, the HMO model has been refined to add a long-term care component for the elderly. This structure, known as the "Social/HMO" (S/HMO) evolved in an attempt to not only reduce costs, but also to improve the appropriateness and quality of care. In the framework of the S/HMO, an attempt is made to achieve these goals by combining somewhat fragmented health and long-term care systems into a single entity—using the same enrollment and prepaid mechanisms found in the typical HMO (Leutz et al., 1988; Abrahams et al., 1989; Newcomer et al., 1990).

Peter Drucker has recently praised the voluntary sector in American life, referring to it as a powerful new counterculture, neither public nor private, which accounts for up to 15 percent of the gross national product. He believes its involvement in hospitals, schools, symphony orchestras, church organizations, colleges, museums, and other settings is significant, and should continue to grow in the future—forging new bonds of community and creating meaningful citizenry (Drucker, 1989).

The evolution of voluntary HSOs in 20th-Century America may thus be summarized as follows:

Pre-1900: The U.S. had a history, since its early colonization, of the provision of limited voluntary service to specific target populations, through mechanisms originally rooted in religious sponsorship, and later secularized through institutions such as the Charity Organization Society. The services provided were often quite limited and sporadic.

1900-1930: The millions of new immigrants in the first several decades of this Century prompted much voluntary effort in the absence of substantial governmental programs. The settlement house movement—largely a product of the efforts of the white middle class, and mutual-aid/self-help societies—formed by immigrants themselves, predominated the voluntary sector (along with the older, religious-sponsored services).

1930-1970: Major systematic focus was brought to the voluntary sector at this time by the establishment of the Family Welfare Association of America and its successor organizations. While the staff of family service agencies have been affected by cyclical psychological/social theories, which vary in their focus on individual versus environmental (internal versus external) factors, the Association did bring significant structure to a major segment of the voluntary human services arena. With the assistance of favorable Federal tax legislation for corporate charitable contributions, voluntary agencies were able to use this period to consolidate fund-raising through umbrella organizations which reached a wider contributor audience.

1970-Present: Increased demand for services, at a time when the gap between the disadvantaged and the middle/upper classes is increasing, has put a great strain upon many voluntary agencies. As government funding has diminished in recent years, so has some private funding through United Way-type organizations. Some agencies have raised their fees, while others have attempted to increase reimbursement from third-party payers, or revenues through contracts with business and industry for employee-related services—discussed below (Minahan, 1987, pp. 591–592). Adding to the problem has been the development of private, for-profit agencies, which have been accused of "skimming the cream" by selective intake, leaving the voluntary agencies with even greater financial instability. Stoesz has suggested that to remain viable in a more competitive welfare industry, the voluntary sector may have to merge independent agencies into oligopolies, or establish nationwide, centrally-controlled franchises of human services agencies (Stoesz, 1989a).

PRIVATE HSOs

The United States has had a limited tradition of providing human services in a for-profit manner, as governmental and voluntary organizations have operated side by side, with shifting emphases, since the beginnings of organized philanthrophy (Macarov, 1991). The earliest involvements of the private sector appear not to have been self-generated, but rather spurred by governmental subsidies. From colonial times until the New Deal of the 1930s, the private sector was more likely to become involved in the human services if governmental financial support were present. In colonial times, awards were granted by governmental authorities to private residents who entered the lowest bids to provide food and shelter to the poor. Physicians also were encouraged to place low bids for the provision of medical care to the poor (Friedlander, 1961).

On the institutional level, private asylums and hospitals gradually replaced home relief in the 1700s and 1800s, as they also received governmental subsidies for caring for the poor (Grob, 1973; Warner, 1971). In addition, a number of private, for-profit hospitals in the 19th century existed to serve the very wealthy for psychiatric or addiction diagnoses. Light traces the major entrance of for-profit firms into the social welfare arena to the 1960s, when Medicare, Medicaid, and the Civilian Health and Medical Program of the Uniform Services (CHAMPUS) were authorized to pay funds to proprietary nursing homes, hospitals, and mental health facilities. Since then, a number of independent, for-profit human services corporations have been created, providing an extensive range of services—including the above-mentioned, as well as health maintenance organizations, child care, home care, life care, and corrections (Light, 1986).

Since 1968, for instance, there has been a burgeoning growth in for-profit hospitals—usually in the form of multihospital chains, such as Hospital Corporation of America and Humana (Brown and Lewis, 1976; Brown and McCool, 1980; Alexander and D'Aunno, 1990; Scarpaci, 1989). At present, approximately 15 percent of the nation's nearly 7000 hospitals are for-profit, investor-owned (Raffel and Raffel, 1989, p. 152). Investor-owned hospital corporations claim they are able to earn a profit because they operate more efficiently than the traditional, more promi-

nent voluntary not-for-profit institutions. They point to superior management specialists, and the ability to enjoy economies of scale through
group purchasing, centralized financing—and related factors. Critics
accuse them of "cream-skimming"—admitting patients on a selective
basis, with less serious medical conditions, who are able to pay the full
costs of their hospitalization, thus reducing outstanding revenues (Haglund
and Dowling, 1988).

Multihospital systems were on the American scene long before the
recent development of for-profit chains. Religious and fraternal groups
had multihospital systems decades before the inroads of the proprietary
sector. In view of the rapid escalation in this area, Zuckerman and Weeks
have pointed out several potential legal problems in this development:
(1) the possibility of governmental charges under the Sherman and
Clayton Acts, which were originally passed to promote free competition
through the avoidance of price-fixing, monopolies, and related activities;
and (2) loss of tax-exempt status among not-for-profit hospitals engaging
in activities which are income-producing, yet viewed by the Internal
Revenue Service as unrelated to their tax-exempt status (Zuckerman and
Weeks, 1979). Perlmutter and Adams recently raised a similar concern
regarding the tax-exempt status of voluntary social agencies which become
involved with profit-making ventures (Perlmutter and Adams, 1990).

Despite these concerns over governmental controls on multihospital
systems, both proprietary and not-for-profit, projections are that soon
half the nation's hospitals will belong to such systems (Bisbee, 1981).

An interesting corollary development in the criminal justice system
has been the entrance of the proprietary sector into the ownership/
management of prisons or selective prison services. Since the mid-1980s,
this phenomenon has been slowly spreading in America (National Institute of Justice, 1985).

In this instance, private vendors either supply the space for inmates,
or take over existing public buildings. Room rates are established—based
on capital investments, operating costs, and expected occupancy. The
government (which may be federal, state or local) is charged by the day
for each detainee. At the local level, there is special interest in detention
services for populations with short terms of confinement—such as illegal
aliens or county prisoners (Wall Street Journal, February 5, 1987).
Sometimes, the contracting private agency will only offer specific in-prison
services, such as medical care, or services to juveniles. In regard to the
latter, by the mid-1980s, there were just over 1800 privately-operated

juvenile residential programs in the United States (Tillett, 1985). As with the proprietary hospital sector discussed above, charges have been made that such corporations will "skim the cream"—offering to contract for minimum-risk inmates, or profitable services only, or will reduce quality by cutting costs. The corporations involved argue that they can improve the quality of service, at reduced costs, because of their management expertise gained in the private sector (Territo et al., 1989; Ring, 1987).

Corrections Corporation of America (CCA), a high-profile player on the scene, was founded in 1983, and has enjoyed continued growth—helped by the commonplace of prison overcrowding and court orders in many states requiring upgrading of corrections systems and alleviation of overcrowding. As a result, a number of states have passed, or are considering passing, legislation which will permit privatization of new and existing correctional facilities. CCA believes it offers six distinct advantages to problems in the corrections industry: (1) professional management; (2) long-range planning; (3) reduced administrative problems; (4) reduced legal liability for the governmental entity contracting with CCA; (5) improved facility design; and (6) reduced capital requirements (Corrections Corporation of America, 1986).

The free-enterprise ethic, revisited during the Reagan Era (1980–1988), is expected by Stoesz to contribute to the continued growth in privatization of human services well into the 1990s. He sees "corporate welfare" as the third stage of welfare in the United States, and points to particularly rapid growth and consolidation in regard to nursing homes, HMOs, child care and home care services. Stoesz expects that the number of private services may come to equal those traditionally offered by not-for-profit agencies (Stoesz, 1986: Stoesz, 1987). In addition to the growth in for-profit health care (most recently proliferating in the provision of specialized care for addiction/substance abuse), and the growth in private management of prisons, he also cites the development of "employee assistance programs" (EAPs), whereby employers in industrial/corporate settings provide human services to workers in need (Stoesz, 1989b; Masi, 1984). It has been reported that 60 percent of the "Fortune 500" companies had EAPs by the mid-1980s (Personnel Journal, 1986). Such programs are generally "sold" to employers in the belief that they are cost-effective; will decrease insurance premiums, errors, and absenteeism; and increase productivity. Such programs can be provided in-house, by human services professionals on the payroll of the employer, or contracted out to private or nonprofit agencies (Straussner, 1988). Ironically,

Landesman and Bucolo report resistance to establishing EAPs in health care settings. They believe the resistance comes from both individual staff members who view themselves as "healthy experts" not in need of treatment, and concerns on the part of hospital administrators that a hospital-based EAP would be cost-prohibitive. Landesman and Bucolo believe, however, that the same benefits (cited above) which accrue to other work settings that support EAPs would apply to health care settings also (Landesman and Bucolo, 1987).

Not all analysts are euphoric over the recent inroads into the human services by the for-profit sector. In a review of the process, Abramovitz argues that privatization channels public dollars into private hands, strengthens the two-class welfare state, and reproduces the inequalities of the free market. She especially fears excessive profits, higher prices, lower wages, fewer workers, weaker unions, and less service for those in need (Abramovitz, 1986).

The evolution of for-profit HSOs in the twentieth century may thus be summarized as follows:

Pre-1900:   There was limited private involvement with the poor and sick, through governmental subsidies, during the early years of this nation. By the nineteenth century, government subsidies diminished the previous emphasis on home care. In the nineteenth and early twentieth centuries, a number of private, exclusive hospitals, serving only the very wealthy, also existed—often for the treatment of mental illness or substance abuse.

1900–1930:   Limited involvement of the proprietary sector in the human services continued, at a slow growth rate.

1930–1970:   Limited involvement of the proprietary sector in the human services continued, at a slow growth rate.

1970–Present: Proliferation of for-profit hospitals and multihospital systems occurred, with slower, but noticeable, development of the proprietary sector in the area of corrections/prisons/detention facilities. Selective admission of patients allegedly occurred in the proprietary hospital sector—often involving those in need of treatment for less serious medical conditions, or treatment for substance abuse/mental illness. A similar development is allegedly emerging in the selection of clientele and services offered by corrections management corporations. In industry, human services are being increasingly provided by employers, to their employees, often through contracts with for-profit (and other) providers.

SUMMARY

As we can see from this brief overview, governmental services evolved after a need was first identified, legislation was eventually passed, and the service needed was provided. The overall governmental approach to most human services in the twentieth century was therefore incremental, often piecemeal. On the voluntary level, needs were identified, and services provided, often long before corresponding supportive legislation. The voluntary sector exhibited earlier sensitivity to the provision of

Table 1. The Evolution of Human Services in the Twentieth Century: Growth; Populations Served: Focus of Services.

	Pre-1900	*1900–1930*	*1930–1970*	*1970–Present*
GROWTH:				
Government	Minimal growth	Growth	Growth	Decline
Voluntary	Limited (primary provider)	Growth	Growth	Growth/increased demand
Private	Limited growth	Limited growth	Some growth	Accelerated growth
POPULATIONS SERVED:				
Government	Public in need of protection	Public in need of protection	Public in need of health services/poor	Public in need of health services/poor
Voluntary	Poor	Immigrants	The family	The family
Private	Poor/wealthy	Poor/wealthy/ sick	Poor/wealthy/ elderly	Continues to broaden
FOCUS OF SERVICES:				
Government	Public in need of protection, food, shelter, medical care	Public in need of protection, health and education	Income maintenance/ social security	Planning/ reimbursing the states for services
Voluntary	Financial need and in-kind services	Settlement house services, social environment, philanthropy	Self-help	HMOs/SHMOs/ EAPs
Private	Food, shelter and medical care	Food, shelter and medical care	Diverse health care services	Health care/ corrections/EAPs

holistic care than did the government. On the private, for-profit level, needs and legislation influenced the provision of selected services, but mainly those needs which were likely to prove profitable, either because of governmental or insurance support, or an affluent clientele.

Table 1 contains a summary of the evolution of human services in the 20th Century, in terms of growth, populations served, and focus of services.

One may well wonder about the significance of this evolutionary process in the lives of Americans as we approach the 21st Century. It is to this issue that we now turn in Part II.

REFERENCES

Abrahams, Ruby, John Capitman, Walter Leutz and Peg Macko. "Variations in Care Planning Practice in the Social/HMO: An Exploratory Study," *The Gerontologist*, Vol. 29, No. 6, 1989, pp. 725–736.

Abramovitz, Mimi. "The Privatization of the Welfare State: A Review," *Social Work*, July–August 1986, pp. 257–264.

Addams, Jane. *Twenty Years at Hull House*. New York: Signet, 1960.

Alcoholics Anonymous World Services. *Twelve Steps and Twelve Traditions*. New York: Alcoholics Anonymous World Services, 1984.

Alexander, Jeffrey A. and Thomas A. D'Aunno. "Transformation of Institutional Environments: Perspectives on the Corporatization of U.S. Health Care," in *Innovation in Health Care Delivery*, Stephen Mick, (ed.)., San Francisco: Jossey-Bass, 1990, Ch. 3, pp. 53–85.

Alperin, Diane. "Family Service Agencies: Responding to Change in a Conservative Decade," To be published in *Families in Society*, 1991.

Anderson, Odin. *HMO Developments: Patterns and Prospects*. Chicago, Pluribus Press, 1985.

Berki, S. et al. "Enrollment Choice in a Multi-HMO Setting: The Roles of Health Risk, Vulnerability and Access to Care," *Medical Care*, Vol. 15, 1977, pp. 95–114.

Bisbee, Gerald, (ed.). *Multihospital Systems: Policy Issues for the Future*. Chicago: Hospital Research and Educational Trust, 1981.

Blumenstein, Henry. "Survival Issues Challenging Family Agencies," *Social Casework*, February 1988, pp. 107–115.

Briggs, John. *An Italian Passage*. New Haven: Yale University Press, 1978.

Brown, Montague and Harold Lewis. *Hospital Management Systems*. Germantown, MD: Aspen Systems, 1976.

Brown, Montague and Barbara McCool. *Multihospital Systems*. Germantown, MD: Aspen Systems, 1980.

Chambliss, William, J. (ed.). *Sociological Readings in the Conflict Perspective*. Reading, MA: Addison-Wesley, 1973.

Committee on the Costs of Medical Care. *Medical Care for the American People*.

Chicago: University of Chicago Press, 1932. Reprinted in 1970 by the U.S.D.H.E.W., Public Health Service, GPO, Washington, DC.

Corrections Corporation of America. *1986 Annual Report.* Nashville, TN: CCA, 1986.

DiNitto, D. and T. Dye. *Social Welfare Politics and Public Policy.* Englewood Cliffs, NJ: Prentice-Hall, 1987.

Donabedian, Avedis. *A Review of Some Experiences with Prepaid Group Practice.* Ann Arbor: Bureau of Public Health Economics, Research Series No. 12, School of Public Health, 1965.

Donabedian, Avedis. *Aspects of Medical Care Administration.* Cambridge, MA: Harvard University Press, 1973.

Drucker, Peter. *The New Realities.* New York: Harper and Row, 1989.

Ellwood, Paul et al. "The Health Maintenance Strategy." Rockville, MD: NCHSR&D, June 25, 1970 (mimeographed).

Engleman, Rose and Robert Joy. *Two Hundred Years of Military Medicine.* Fort Detrick, MD: U.S. Army Medical Department, 1975.

Epstein, Charlotte. *An Introduction to the Human Services.* Englewood Cliffs, New Jersey: Prentice-Hall, 1981.

Feingold, Eugene, (ed.). *Medicare: Policy and Politics.* San Francisco: Chandler, 1966.

Fenno, Richard. *The President's Cabinet.* Cambridge: Harvard University Press, 1959.

Flexner, Abraham. *Medical Education in the United States and Canada.* New York: The Carnegie Foundation, 1910.

Friedlander, W.A. *Introduction to Social Welfare.* Englewood Cliffs, New Jersey: Prentice-Hall, 1961, pp. 68–70.

Friedman, Milton. *Capitalism and Freedom.* Chicago: University of Chicago Press, 1963.

Garfield, Sidney. "The Delivery of Medical Care," *Scientific American,* Vol. 222, No. 4, April 1970, pp. 15–23.

Gartner, A. and F. Riessman. *The Self-Help Revolution.* New York: Human Sciences Press, 1984.

Ginsberg, Leon. "Social Work and the 1988 Elections," *Social Work,* Vol. 34, No. 2, March 1989, pp. 161–166.

Glazer, N. "The Social Policy of the Reagan Administration: A Review," *The Public Interest,* Vol. 75, 1984, pp. 76–98.

Grob, G.N. *Mental Institutions in America: Social Policy to 1985.* New York: Free Press, 1973.

Gumbiner, Robert. *HMO: Putting it All Together.* St. Louis, Mo: C.V. Mosby, 1975.

Gutek, Gerald. *An Historical Introduction to American Education.* New York: Harper and Row, 1970.

Haglund, Claudia and William Dowling. "The Hospital," in *Introduction to Health Services,* Stephen Williams and Paul Torrens, (eds.). 3rd Edition. New York: John Wiley, 1988, Ch. 6, pp. 160–211.

Hasenfeld, Yeheskel and Richard A. English (eds.). *Human Service Organizations: A Book of Readings.* Ann Arbor, MI: The University of Michigan Press, 1974.

Hyman, Herbert. *Health Planning: A Systematic Approach.* Germantown, MD: Aspen Systems, 1976.

Jansson, B. *Theory and Practice of Social Welfare Policy.* Belmont, CA: Wadsworth, 1984.

Jimenez, Mary Ann. "Historical Evolution and Future Challenges of the Human Services Professions," *Families in Society: The Journal of Contemporary Human Services,* Vol. 71, No. 1, January 1990, pp. 3–12.

Johnson, H. Wayne. *The Social Services: An Introduction.* Itasca, IL: F.E. Peacock, 1986.

Kahn, Ernest. "The Voluntary Sector Can Remain Alive—and Well," in *Human Services at Risk,* Felice Perlmutter, (ed.). Lexington, MA: Lexington Books, 1984, Ch. 4, pp. 57–74.

Kohlert, Nancy. "Welfare Reform: A Historic Consensus," *Social Work,* Vol. 34, No. 4, July 1989, pp. 303–306.

Landesman, Toby and Joseph Bucolo. "EAPs in Health Care," *EAP Digest,* January/February 1987, pp. 37–39.

Lee, Philip. "Do We Need a Federal Department of Health?," in *Politics of Health,* Douglass Cater and Philip Lee, (eds.)., New York: Medcom Press, 1972.

Lee, Philip and A.E. Benjamin. "Health Policy and the Politics of Health Care," in *Introduction to Health Services,* Stephen Williams and Paul Torrens, (eds.). 3rd Edition. New York: John Wiley, 1988, Ch. 15, pp. 457–479.

Leiby, J. *A History of Social Welfare and Social Work in the United States.* New York: Columbia University Press, 1978.

Leutz, Walter, R. Abrahams, M. Greenlick, R. Kane, J. Prottas. "Targeting Expanded Care to the Aged: Early SHMO Experience," *The Gerontologist,* Vol. 28, No. 1, 1988, pp. 4–17.

Light, D. "Corporate Medicine for Profit," *Scientific American,* Vol. 255, 1986, pp. 38–45.

Luce, Brown. "Medical Technology and Its Assessment," in *Introduction to Health Services,* Stephen Williams and Paul Torrens, (eds.). 3rd Edition. New York: John Wiley, 1988, Ch. 9, pp. 281–307.

Macarov, David. *Certain Change: Social Work Practice in the Future.* Silver Spring, MD: National Association of Social Workers, 1991.

Marmor, Theodore, Jerry Mashaw and Philip Harvey. *America's Misunderstood Welfare State: Persistant Myth, Enduring Realities.* New York: Basic Books, 1990.

Martin, G. *Social Policy in the Welfare State.* Englewood Cliffs, NJ: Prentice-Hall, 1990.

Masi, D. *Designing Employee Assistance Programs.* New York: Amacon, 1984.

Minahan, Anne (ed.). *Encyclopedia of Social Work—18th Edition.* Silver Spring, MD: National Association of Social Workers, 1987.

Miringoff, Marc. *Management in Human Service Organizations.* New York: Macmillan, 1980.

Morris, Robert. *Rethinking Social Welfare.* New York: Longman, 1986.

Mowbray, Albert and Ralph Blanchard. *Insurance.* New York: McGraw-Hill, 1955.

Mullan, Fitzhugh. *Plagues and Politics: The Story of the United States Public Health Service.* New York: Basic Books, 1989.

National Institute of Justice. *Corrections and the Private Sector.* Washington, DC: U.S. Department of Justice, May 1985.

Newcomer, Robert, Charlene Harrington and Alan Friedlob. "Awareness and Enrollment in the Social/HMO," *The Gerontologist,* Vol. 30, No. 1, 1990, pp. 86–93.

Pancoast, D., P. Parker and C. Froland. *Rediscovering Self-Help: Its Role in Social Care.* Beverly Hills, CA: Sage, 1983.

Perlmutter, F. and C. Adams. "The Voluntary Sector and For-Profit Ventures: The Transformation of American Social Welfare?", *Administration in Social Work,* Vol. 14, No. 1, 1990, pp. 1–13.

Perrow, Charles. "Hospitals: Technology, Structure and Goals," in *Handbook of Organizations,* James G. March (ed.). Chicago: Rand McNally, 1965, pp. 910–971.

Personnel Journal. "Employee Assistance—an EAP Update: A Perspective for the 1980s," *Personnel Journal,* June 1986.

Powell, T. *Self-Help Organizations and Professional Practice.* Silver Spring, MD: National Association of Social Workers, 1987.

Public Law 79–725, *Hospital Survey and Construction Act* (Hill-Burton), 1946, U.S. Congress.

Public Law 79–487, *National Mental Health Act,* 1946, U.S. Congress.

Public Law 89–239, *Heart Disease, Cancer and Stroke Amendments of 1965,* 1965, U.S. Congress.

Public Law 89-749, *Comprehensive Health Planning and Public Health Service Amendments of 1966,* 1966, U.S. Congress.

Public Law 93-222. *The Health Maintenance Organization Act,* 1973, U.S. Congress.

Public Law 93-641, *National Health Planning and Resources Development Act of 1974,* 1974, U.S. Congress.

Raffel, Marshall and Norma Raffel. *The U.S. Health System: Origins and Functions—3rd Edition.* New York: John Wiley, 1989.

Rice, Robert. "Change and Continuity in Family Services," *Families in Society: The Journal of Contemporary Human Services,* 1990, pp. 24–31.

Richie, Nicholas. "Health Planning—An Overview," *American Journal of Health Planning,* Vol. 3, No. 5, April 1978, pp. 36–42.

Richmond, Mary. *Friendly Visiting Among the Poor: Handbook for Charity Workers.* New York: Macmillan, 1899.

Richmond, Mary. *Social Diagnosis.* New York: Russell Sage Foundation, 1917.

Riessman, F. "Forward," in *Self-Help Organizations and Professional Practice.* Silver Spring, MD: National Association of Social Workers, 1987, pp. vii–x.

Riley, P. "Family Services," in *Handbook of the Social Sciences,* N. Gilbert and H. Sprecht (eds.). Englewood Cliffs, New Jersey: Prentice-Hall, 1981, Chapter 5, pp. 82–101.

Ring, Charles. "Private Prisons Need a Fair Trial," *The Wall Street Journal,* Vol. 109, May 8, 1987, p. 22.

Rosen, George. *A History of Public Health.* New York: MD Publications, 1958.

Scarpaci, Joseph L., (ed.). *Health Services Privatization in Industrial Societies.* New Brunswick, NJ: Rutgers University Press, 1989.

Schiro, George. *Americans by Choice.* New York: Arno Press, 1975.

Shonick, William. "Public Health Services: Background and Present Status," in *Introduction to Health Services,* Stephen Williams and Paul Terrens, (eds.). 3rd Edition. New York: John Wiley, 1988, Ch. 4, pp. 85–123.

Silverman, P. *Mutual Help Groups and the Role of the Mental Health Professional.* DHEW Publication No. ADM 78–646. Washington, DCV: Government Printing Office, 1978.

Social Security Act of 1935, 42 U.S. Code, Section 301.

Stanfield, Peggy. *Introduction to the Health Professions.* Boston: Jones and Bartlett, 1990.

Stein, Shayna, Margaret Linn, Jacqueline Edelstein and Elliot Stein. "Elderly Patients' Satisfaction with Care Under HMO Versus Private Systems," *Southern Medical Journal,* Vol. 82, No. 1, January 1989, pp. 3–8.

Stern, Mark. "The Politics of American Social Welfare," in *Human Services at Risk,* Felice Perlmutter, (ed.). Lexington, MA: Lexington Books, 1984, Ch. 1, pp. 3–21.

Stoesz, David. "Corporate Welfare: The Third Stage of Welfare in the United States," *Social Work,* July–August 1986, pp. 245–249.

Stoesz, David. "Privatization: Reforming the Welfare State," *Journal of Sociology and Social Welfare,* Vol. 14, No. 3, 1987, pp. 3–19.

Stoesz, David. "Functional Conception of Social Work," *Social Work,* Vol. 33, 1988, pp. 58–59.

Stoesz, David. "A Theory of Social Welfare," *Social Work,* Vol. 34, No. 2, 1989a, 101–107.

Stoesz, David. "Human Service Corporations: New Opportunities for Administration in Social Work," *Administration in Social Work,* Vol. 13, No. 3/4, 1989b, pp. 183–197.

Straussner, S.L. "Comparison of In-House and Contracted-Out Employee Assistance Programs," *Social Work,* Vol. 33, 1988, pp. 53–55.

Territo, Leonard, James Halsted and Max Bromley. *Crime and Justice in America.* St. Paul, MN: West, 1989.

Tillett, D.C. *Private Jails — Contracting Out Public Service.* Lexington, KY: Council of State Governments, 1985.

Traunstein, Donald. "From Mutual-Aid Self-Help To Professional Service," *Social Casework: The Journal of Contemporary Social Work,* December 1984, pp. 622–627.

Turner, Jonathan. *The Structure of Sociological Theory.* 3rd Edition. Homewood, IL: Dorsey Press, 1982.

U.S. Department of Health, Education and Welfare. *Trends Affecting the U.S. Health Care System.* Washington, DC: Government Printing Office, January, 1976.

Wall Street Journal, "Review and Outlook: Prisons for Profit," *The Wall Street Journal,* Vol. 109, February 15, 1987, p. 20.

Warner, A. *American Charities.* New York: Russell and Russell, 1894 — reprinted in 1971.

Wenocur, Stanley and Michael Reisch. *From Charity to Enterprise: The Development of American Social Work in a Market Economy.* Chicago: University of Illinois Press, 1989.

Wilensky, Harold and Charles Lebeaux. *Industrial Society and Social Welfare.* New York: Russell Sage Foundation, 1958.

Willen, M. "Parents Anonymous: The Professionals' Role as Sponsor," in *The Self-Help Revolution,* A. Gartner and F. Reissman, (eds.). New York: Human Sciences Press, 1984, pp. 109–119.

Wilson, Florence and Duncan, Neuhauser. *Health Services in the United States.* Cambridge, MA: Ballinger, 1976.

Zuckerman, Howard and Lewis Weeks. *Multi-Institutional Hospital Systems.* Chicago: Hospital Research and Educational Trust, 1979.

PART II

HUMAN SERVICES FOR THE NINETIES

TRENDS IN THE 1990s

Predicting the future is a risky business. However, that has never prevented individuals from so doing (Bell, 1973). In fact, Macarov points out several advantages to human service workers who attempt to predict the future—including the ability to plan accordingly, anticipate situations which will require professional intervention, identify outmoded behaviors (cultural lag), and influence the direction the future takes (Macarov, 1991). In recent years, futurology and trend analysis have gained increasing popularity, and perhaps no one has received wider publicity in this area than John Naisbitt, author of *Megatrends* (Naisbitt, 1982) and coauthor of *Megatrends 2000* (Naisbitt and Aburdene, 1990).

In the former volume, Naisbitt focused on the trend from an industrial society to an information society, as does Toffler in a recent work (Toffler, 1990), in which technology must be counterbalanced by a human response (i.e., "high touch"). As we move from a national economy to a global one, he sees a shift from short-term to long-term goals, and from centralization to decentralization. On the individual level, he observes a trend away from institutional help and toward self-help, instead. Greater participatory democracy is expected, through "networking" (where people are not encumbered by large bureaucracies, but rather interact directly with one another, sharing ideas, information, resources). In the midst of all these developments, he sees a shift from "either-or" to "multiple-options" (Naisbitt, 1982).

As we approach the year 2000, Naisbitt and Aburdene succumb to the historical tendency to speculate on the forthcoming new century/new millenium in their book, *Megatrends 2000* (Naisbitt and Aburdene, 1990). Of particular relevance to our focus here is their vision of the emergence of free-market socialism, in which human service needs will be met/ provided by the increasing involvement of the private sector. They point

30

to recent developments in Eastern Europe as examples of decentralization/ deregulation by governments and the privatization of the Welfare State (e.g., in the United Kingdom under Margaret Thatcher). Accompanying this movement is a set of new values/new policies—principal among them, that of "workfare," which embodies the belief that people are better off working than depending on government resources (Kohlert, 1989). Also included in this approach is the view that a new social contract has emerged, in which people who accept welfare benefits owe the government a good-faith attempt to get a job. Implicit in this redirection is a belief on the part of some that the people the "Welfare State" sought to assist were worse off in 1980 than *before* the Great Society programs (Murray, 1984). One consequence of such changes is that many human service agencies are faced with conflicting, contradictory ideologies today, and are viewed ambivalently by the public (Brager and Holloway, 1978). Day urges those in the human services to formulate long-range policies, in order to cope with the dynamic changes occurring at this time. In particular, she urges: (1) that human services professionals must guard against changes that may eliminate or decrease necessary programs/ services; (2) that they sponsor/support new programs to aid clients through the difficult times to come; and (3) that they adopt an "activist mode," geared to social action/social change (Day, 1989).

In the midst of these recent developments, Atherton has suggested that the "liberals" who have traditionally played a major role in the provision of human services, need to: (1) shed their naive view that "The Government" is necessarily a beneficent entity; (2) find some central direction for their agenda—that pulls together the many disparate factions/interests in their camp; and (3) accept the fact that the idea of a paternalistic redistributive "State" is an idea whose time has gone, much the same way as central government economic planning and public ownership of the means of production (Atherton, 1990).

Stoesz and Karger have also entered the fray, discussing recent changes in social values/philosophy in America. Since the early 1980s, they have observed a "loose alliance" of religious fundamentalists and conservative populists forming an influential traditionalist movement, which seeks to reinforce such basic values as: respect for family and country, hard work, freedom, and independence. This loose coalition espouses that human welfare programs have eroded the work ethic and encouraged undesirable behavior. Its potency was felt in the 1980 presidential campaign and the election of Ronald Reagan (Stoesz and Karger, 1990).

Stoesz and Karger go on to compare "neo-conservative" and "neo-liberal" positions on human welfare programs. The neo-conservative position is characterized by: (1) a reaffirmation of a "need-only" philosophy; (2) an increased effort to eliminate fraud; (3) the establishment of workfare; (4) removal of inappropriate clients from service rolls; (5) enforcing support of dependents by those responsible; (6) improving the efficiency of human services administration; and (7) a shifting of responsibility from the federal government to state and local entities, and private institutions. The neo-liberal position is characterized by: (1) disenchantment over the perceived failure of the means-tested programs of the War on Poverty that were implemented in the 1960s; (2) a desire to reduce governmental costs by encouraging businesses to assume more responsibility for the welfare of the population—for instance, through giving government grants to businesses which agree to hire the chronically unemployed, provide child care for workers, disability and unemployment benefits, and relocation assistance; (3) using human welfare programs to rebuild deteriorating communities—for which there are New Deal precedents, such as the Civilian Conservation Corps, Works Progress Administration, and Public Works Administration; and (4) justifying new social programs by stressing that they are "investments" in human capital (Stoesz and Karger, 1990).

The emphasis Naisbitt and Aburdene place on the individual in the 1990s, as the foundation of society—free to be responsible, creative, and self-fulfilling, echoes a recent theme of Peter Drucker. Drucker pays homage to the significant "third sector" (in addition to the public/governmental and private/proprietary sectors). This third sector is comprised of the large numbers of volunteers in the U.S. who seek individual self-fulfillment in areas of interest, while at the same time alleviating human suffering and making cultural and other contributions through donated time, talent, and money. As Drucker sees it, many of these volunteers are involved in "human change institutions," whose roots are in the 18th-Century Enlightenment Movement (Drucker, 1989).

The authors of this volume, after reviewing the work of Naisbitt, Drucker, and others, and considering the historical issues discussed in PART I, conclude that in the coming decade, certain factors/trends will impact heavily upon the human services—whether provided by government, volunteers, or the proprietary sector. This impact will be largely in terms of "innovation," a concept which has several definitions. One definition refers to "invention," whereby a creative process occurs to produce new phenomena. Another definition refers to the process of "adoption" of changes which are new to organizations and their relevant environments (Steinhauer, 1988). Both definitions are utilized in this discussion, and the following trends are expected to have major consequences:

1. ***The United States will continue to have a "mixed economy".*** There is little evidence to lead one to believe that the American people as a whole, or the majority of their elected representatives, are ready to dismantle the health/education/welfare/criminal justice involvements of the government (at various levels) in the lives of citizens. Surely, budgetary cuts and attempts to control deficits—as well as changes in administrations and their philosophies, will continue the periodic "contractions" in governmental involvement in the human services. But, these are expected to be followed by cyclical periods of expansion—if only in selected areas (the history of developed societies reflects the processes of action/counteraction as they swing from one view to another, in an attempt to achieve balance/homeostasis). It is also equally unlikely that the United States is ready to adopt a full-scale socialist model in the near future. With the recent high-profile failure of socialism in Eastern Europe, the more moderate "free-market socialism" mentioned earlier will likely have a chance to play itself out in the coming decade or two, during and after which an assessment can be made regarding its future viability.

2. ***The disparity between the poor and the rest of society will likely widen in the coming decade.*** The "underclass," plagued by a "culture of poverty," including chronic unemployment, a long history of public assistance, out-of-wedlock teenage pregnancy, drug/alcohol addictions, and numerous medical problems (including AIDS) is not likely to quickly go away (Lewis, 1959; Harrington, 1962). Reischauer defines America's underclass as "a class of people who are outside the nation's economic, and social mainstream, a group that has no significant stake in our current political system" (Reischauer, 1987, p. 27). Wilson has recently argued that the existence of the American underclass is mainly due to a *declining economy*, rather than to the failures of the welfare system or the effects of racism (Wilson, 1990). And Day believes that class polarization will result from the widening of the economic gap between the poor and the wealthy. She sees the middle class as moving into a lower standard of living due to unemployment, lower wages, and an increase in the number of single-parent families. At the same time, people of wealth are less

often investing in either the human or productive resources of the United States (Day, 1989).

The Bureau of the Census reports that in 1988, the poverty threshold for a family of four was $12,092, and 31.9 million people (13.1% of the population) were in poverty (U.S. Department of Commerce, Bureau of the Census, 1990, p. 458). No solution has yet been found to provide the comprehensive, coordinated human services needed by these individuals.

3. *The population will continue to "age".* In 1960, life expectancy at birth was 66.6 years for males and 73.1 for females. In 1990, the respective figures were 72.1 and 79 (U.S. Department of Commerce, Bureau of the Census, 1990, p. 72). Fewer and fewer working-age individuals will be left to support the elderly—who will present a host of economic/social/cultural/medical problems. The demands of the elderly in the next several decades will make it extremely difficult to fund a new "War on Poverty" (Stern, 1984).

4. *Technology will continue to develop in ways that impact our lives, both in a positive and negative manner.* While technological advances carry hope for the resolution of many vexing problems, they also hold the potential for causing frustration on at least two levels: (a) some problems cannot be solved by technology, or at least not as quickly as desired (e.g., the AIDS crisis); and (b) technology may create problems unknown in less-sophisticated times (e.g., prolongation of the dying process). On the other hand, to the extent that technology can assist in the diagnosis, treatment, coordination of human problems, it has great potential for positive use. Lewis Mumford warned some time ago of the "downside" of technology—in terms of the creation of pollution, waste products, and the potential for mass destruction (Mumford, 1967; Mumford, 1970). McNearney illustrated the two-edged sword of technology, in regard to health care in particular, when he listed the positive benefits of health care technology to include a direct effect upon prevention, primary care, institutionalized care and rehabilitation. On the problematic side, he listed cost inflation through the proliferation of new techniques/devices/products, and increased specialization—with all its attendant problems of coordination (McNearney, 1972).

5. *Global developments—in terms of economic interdependency, shared political/cultural/social structures, and communication/transportation interaction, will make universal suffering much more visible.* The need for human services abroad, as well as at home, will raise questions about the

universality of humanity, our mutual dependence on a pollution-free planet, and the allocation of resources at home and abroad (through foreign aid, cost-sharing, etc.). Hartman cites the interrelatedness of economic, social, political, domestic, international, and ecological issues when referring to the fact that "we have come to live.... in a global village" (Hartman, 1990, p. 291). In periods of economic recession, isolationist groups may gain increased membership and visibility. However, responsible governments, recognizing the commonality of the human condition, will endeavor to strike a balance between ethnocentric needs at home, and those of an increasingly-interdependent world community.

With such macrosystem variables, as the above, impacting on the human services sector in the 1990s, it is appropriate to review what is likely to be occurring on the individual, or microsystem, level. It is to this issue that we now turn.

COMMON HUMAN NEEDS IN THE 1990s

In her classic monograph, Charlotte Towle articulated the needs common to all human beings. The most basic impulse, to survive, is accompanied by the need for physical welfare, emotional growth, development of intellectual capacity, spiritual needs, the need to be loved/cared for/secure, the need for economic security, and the need to be creative (Towle, 1965).

Maslow later related need to motivation, postulating a "hierarchy of needs" which dictates an individual's strivings and behavior. At the most basic level are physiological needs (such as hunger, thirst), followed by security, social needs, self-esteem and self-actualization. The latter refers to a level of functioning where the individual is operating at full capacity/full satisfaction in the quest to utilize all his/her potential (Maslow, 1970).

Certainly the history of human services in the United States, summarized in Part I of this volume, illustrates the evolving recognition (on the part of governmental, voluntary, and private agencies) of the needs common to all, and the impact of those needs on motivation—through means-tests, workfare, volunteerism, training programs—and other mechanisms.

The Ford Foundation recently sponsored a project to consider the issue of "Social Welfare and the American Future" (Ford Foundation, 1989). A major question that was addressed was whether the momentum established by the Social Security Act of 1935—and the subsequent federal involvement in the human services—could be made more responsive to the common human needs discussed above, or whether more-fundamental change is required to meet the human welfare challenges of the twenty-first century. Participants in the Project recommended that social welfare policy in the U.S. must undergo fundamental reform and modernization, because of major changes in economic, democratic and social conditions. A substantial recommendation of the participants was that the various groups involved in the human services must stop allowing themselves to be pitted one against the other. They call for a social policy that addresses the common human needs of all citizens, and is related to each of the four stages of the life cycle, and the respective problems therein, as follows:

1. **Infancy and Childhood** —where the major problems/issues include: poverty; out-of-wedlock births; child abuse; neglect; prenatal care; nutrition; preschool programs; day care; and child welfare services. Particular attention needs to be paid in this stage to improving the lives of infants and young children in impoverished homes.

2. **Young Adulthood** —where the major problems/issues include: school dropouts; educational incentives; school-based reforms; collaborations between schools and businesses; remedial education; work experience; life-options services; summer training programs; and teenage pregnancy. Particular attention needs to be paid here to easing the transition from school to work for poor adolescents and young adults.

3. **The Working Years** —where the major problems/issues include: economic growth; improving the return to work; assuring health care coverage; redesigning unemployment and welfare programs; and community programs. Particular attention needs to be paid here to enhancing opportunities and securing protection for Americans of working age.

4. **Old Age** —where the major problems/issues include: protecting the weakest among the elderly; rescuing/sustaining Medicare; and creating structures for affordable long-term care. Particular attention needs to be paid here to enhancing protection of the aged and their families.

When these common human needs are not met by existing HSOs, a variety of processes are available by which agencies which can fulfill such unmet needs may come into being. It is to this issue that we now turn.

EXAMPLES OF NEW HSOs

Felice Perlmutter (Perlmutter, 1969) has developed a theoretical model of social agency evolution in which there are three main stages, with the following characteristics:

STAGE 1: SELF-INTEREST —where there is an obvious social problem which the agency seeks to address, through high involvement of Board members in delivering services to the victims of the social problem, via a centralized authority structure.

STAGE 2: PROFESSIONALISM —where the obvious social problem is abated, due to professional staff involvement taking precedence over the Board's involvement, through decentralization of authority, and through categorizing the client population for better service.

STAGE 3: SOCIAL INTEREST —where new, but related, problems are faced by a board and staff which can enjoy "equal" status, and even greater decentralization of authority allows both the original and new target groups to be served.

In the past several decades, the United States has witnessed the evolution of several "new" human services agencies, which offer an opportunity to look at the evolutionary process behind each. We will now turn to examining those processes for four such services—hospices for the terminally ill; continuing/life care facilities for the elderly; community AIDS agencies; and domestic assault shelters.

Hospices for the Terminally Ill

While hospices for the terminally ill were first established in the United States in the early 1970s (Cohen, 1979), the modern movement originated a decade earlier, in Great Britain, primarily through the efforts of a single individual—Dr. Cicely Saunders, who founded St. Christopher's Hospice in London (Buckingham, 1983).

Impetus for the hospice movement came from a variety of sources. There were people working within the health care system (such as the authors of this volume, both former clinical social workers) who were concerned over the treatment of the terminally ill in hospitals. In the not-too-distant past, it was not uncommon to "ignore" terminally-ill patients, except for *mandatory* feeding, medication, and care, and to isolate such individuals—even in the absence of a contagious disease. Staff, including physicians, were ignorant of, and uncomfortable with, death and the dying process, and their encounters with patients reflected this dilemma.

The appearance of Dr. Elisabeth Kubler-Ross' landmark work on death and dying made it easier to conceptualize the dying process, and opened the door to honest discussions of this largely-taboo subject. Continuing education workshops for professionals began to proliferate, during which they were able to openly discuss their own feelings/attitudes, and how the latter impacted on the care they rendered patients (Kubler-Ross, 1970; Everglades Area Health Education Center, 1989).

In the early 1970s, the hospice message slowly spread from community to community, and often a single individual or small group, was responsible for establishing a Board to shepherd the new agency through incorporation. Much of the early work involved educating both health professionals and the public about the hospice philosophy—which emphasizes patient autonomy, palliative care, pain control, and comfort, in a nonthreatening "homey" environment. A variety of settings evolved for hospices in the United States—including specialized wards in hospitals, home health agencies, and free-standing independent hospices with home and/or inpatient care (Hamilton and Reid, 1980). Growth was especially rapid in the 1980s, and according to the National Hospice Organization, there are currently approximately 1600 hospices in the United States (National Hospice Organization, 1990).

Harrison and Richie have described the evolution of a not-for-profit, independent, home-health hospice during its first decade. As a case study, their report has the usual limitations on generalizability common to all case studies. However, the authors note that, "Although demographic, historic, and economic factors cause each hospice to develop uniquely, it is likely that the hospice movement must confront certain common issues and problems regardless of differences in location, organization and sponsorship" (Harrison and Richie, 1988, p. 43).

In examining the first decade of a Florida-based hospice, Harrison and Richie found four "phases" of development, each with its attendant activities and problems, as follows:

Phase 1—Genesis (1978 to early 1979). During this phase, the hospice message was brought back to the community by a single individual who had attended an out-of-state hospice conference. She then recruited a small core of community members with whom she shared the hospice philosophy, and who joined her in establishing the hospice and preparing articles of incorporation. Major problems during this period included finding sufficient lay and medical interest and support, locating office space, and sufficient funds to hire personnel.

Phase 2—The Early Years (late 1979 to 1983). During this phase, considerable public education was needed to explain the hospice philosophy, generate funds, develop relations with community agencies, establish procedures/policies, and obtain state licensure. Major problems at this time included overcoming resistance from the lay and medical communities (in particular, some confused the hospice movement with "active euthanasia," and some physicians and hospitals perceived an economic threat from a new competing agency). Establishing a viable financial base and complying with state licensure requirements were also problematic.

Phase 3—Maturation (1983-1985). During this phase, the agency reached a level of daily functioning that was relatively smooth, allowing for more focus to be placed on long-term goals. Thus, considerable attention was paid to designing a new inpatient facility (to augment the home care available to date), raising funds to construct the building, and processing a certificate-of-need for such a facility. Medicare reimbursement was made available during this period, and certification for it was obtained by the agency. Major problems during this phase included adjusting to the impact of an increasing patient load upon all phases of agency operation, coping with the requirements of Medicare and the certificate-of-need process, developing more-stringent quality control measures, and providing support activities to deal with staff burnout and stress.

Phase 4—Expansion (1985-1988). During this period the caseload had grown so large that the target area was divided into two districts, with separate Patient Care Teams for each. Contracts were established with area nursing homes, in order to serve terminally-ill nursing home patients, and the new inpatient facility neared completion. Major problems included adjusting the agency's organizational structure to its expanded activities, overseeing construction of the new inpatient building—which included compliance with zoning and other regulations, and attempting to establish a broader financial base that would be less dependent upon Medicare.

Today, hospices are a significant factor on the American scene, in the treatment of the terminally ill. Those interested in the movement continue to raise a series of questions regarding licensure, accreditation, financing, evaluation of quality, ethics, and public policy. All these issues are researchable and worthy of further attention (Torrens, 1985; Richie, 1987).

Continuing/Life Care for the Elderly

Another "new" service which came into its own in the past decade or so was the "continuing/life care" facility for the elderly. In their most idealistic form, such facilities have the potential to provide a holistic solution to the multifaceted concerns/problems of the elderly—which include safety, security, health care, and social concerns (Gulick, 1979).

The U.S. population is clearly aging, as data cited earlier indicate. In 1988, over 12 percent of the U.S. population was 65 years of age or older (U.S. Department of Commerce, 1990, p. 13), and in Florida—which is the state with the greatest proportion of residents in this age group, the corresponding figure was over 18 percent (Bureau of Economic and Business Research, 1988, p. 18). While there are differences among the individuals in such a large group, common concerns tend to focus on their safety and security in a sometimes hostile society, economic stability on a fixed income, a place to live, social isolation, and health care needs (Butler, 1975).

The typical arrangement in continuing/life care facilities is that upon payment of an entrance endowment (which may or may not be refundable, in whole or in part), the resident receives an apartment for personal use. This allows for a degree of independent living, while at the same time receiving a variety of social and recreational services (on-site), some meals, and skilled nursing care. The overwhelming majority of over 300 continuing care retirement communities identified by the American Association of Retired Persons were established by nonprofit organizations and community groups, such as churches and fraternal groups, who endeavored to serve their older members. However, private individuals and corporations are entering the field also, creating communities in which they hold equity (Raper, 1984).

Like the hospice movement (discussed above), the continuing/life care movement represents an attempt to find a better solution to the problems of a particular client population, than previously existed. The pressures which contributed to this solution came from the elderly themselves, their caretakers, and legislators concerned with the problems of the elderly. Some research indicates that residents of these communities are often middle or upper-income senior citizens, in their eighties, attempting to fully prepare for the prospect of illness requiring skilled nursing care (Rose, 1983). Research also indicates a variety of social service needs to be met by professional social workers in such settings, because of the multiple problems facing the elderly (Alperin and Richie, 1988).

An area of special concern regarding continuing/life care has been the wide variation in contracts/services from one facility to another. Elderly individuals may not be fully aware of the services covered at their facility, and may find the arrangement less "holistic" than they believed at the time of entrance. A study of continuing/life care facilities in Florida examined the extent to which 23 such facilities offered the following eight services, considered to constitute an appropriate "continuum of care" for residents: emergency call service; skilled nursing home care; at least one prepared meal daily; assistance-in-living; social service for apartment residents; social service for those in the nursing home; home health care; and shelter care. Only one of the 23 facilities studied offered all eight services. Sixty-five percent of the sample offered at least six of the eight. Service seemed to be most infrequent where it was needed to provide a half-way sheltered facility for residents to avoid nursing-home placement—when staying in one's independent residential unit was not recommended. In addition, the availability of home health care services in the residential unit was also identified by only slightly more than half the sample. Services appeared to be clustered at two extreme locations (the resident's apartment and the skilled nursing home) rather than at discrete points on the proposed continuum. The authors of the report recommended that individuals interested in continuing/life care examine very closely all life care contracts before signing, to be sure the range of desired services is actually available at the facility (Alperin and Richie, 1990). It may also be wise to request a financial statement on the prospective agency, prior to signing a contract, as at least one major certified accounting firm has raised questions about the ability of such facilities to keep the lifetime promises made in the contracts (Curran, 1983).

The problems of the elderly are universal, despite differences across cultures and nations, and a variety of models for dealing with these problems are being tried worldwide. One would expect additional new developments in the United States as the population continues to age (Schwab, 1989).

AIDS Services Agencies

In December 1981, *The New England Journal of Medicine* published its first report on a cluster of four men with symptoms which would later become known as Acquired Immune Deficiency Syndrome—AIDS (Gottleib et al., 1981). Since that time, the number of identified cases has risen dramatically worldwide, and by the end of April 1991 in the United States alone, physicians and health departments were reporting almost 170,000 cases meeting the surveillance definition for AIDS (Centers for Disease Control, 1991, p. 5). The World Health Organization (WHO) estimates there have been 1.3 million cases of AIDS worldwide up to the beginning of 1991, and that at least 8-to-10 million adults are infected with the virus. By the turn of the century, WHO estimates that there will be a cumulative total of possibly 30 million people who have been infected, two-thirds of whom will be adults, and the remainder infants and children (World Health Organization, 1991).

The initial focus upon homosexual males, in the early years of this crisis, has shifted as epidemiological data on human immunodeficiency virus (HIV) infection have shown that the number of AIDS cases are increasing disproportionately among certain racial/ethnic minority groups. Blacks, who make up approximately 12 percent of the U.S. population, represent 27 percent of the diagnosed AIDS cases. Hispanics, who only represent 8 percent of the U.S. population, make up 16 percent of persons-with-AIDS. Excluding U.S. territories, the cumulative incidence of AIDS per 100,000 persons is highest in blacks and Hispanics (83.8 and 73.0, respectively—followed by whites at 26.3). Black and Hispanic women and children are also overrepresented. Fifty-seven percent of adult women with AIDS are black, 17 percent are Hispanic, and only 25 percent are white. Of all the children with AIDS, 54 percent are black, 21 percent are Hispanic, and 24 percent are white (Centers for Disease Control, 1990, pp. 3–4).

Since its initial identification, evidence has increasingly mounted regarding the wide-ranging impact of this illness. A systematic analysis cannot ignore the social, legal, political, economic, spiritual, and other components which need to be addressed in order to promote a holistic view of the problem and its potential solutions. A recent multifaceted history of the AIDS experience in America, up to 1988, underscored charges made in both professional and lay publications regarding failure to bring to bear the most potent resources in the medical and governmental sectors early in the epidemic, due to a combination of clinical ignorance, limited resources, and the lack of political power on the part of minority groups initially identified as the target populations (Shilts, 1988).

Alperin and Richie surveyed a nationwide sample of 108 "community AIDS services agencies" (as distinct from "hospital-based" facilities). Among other things, they were interested in knowing the origin of these agencies in the "era of indifference" described by Shilts, when he discussed the relationship between the Reagan Era and the AIDS crisis (Shilts, 1988). They found that the "typical" agency of this type was voluntary, not-for-profit, nonsectarian, and free-standing (not part of another facility/organization). They generally started out as AIDS support groups, founded on a self-help/mutual-aid basis in the mid-1980s, and *later* evolved into more complex entities—funded largely through government grants and donations. The predominant services offered were AIDS information and referral to other agencies. However, a wide range of services was offered, including AIDS testing, food banks, clothing banks, respite care, transportation, legal assistance, meals-on-wheels, and others (Alperin and Richie, 1989).

The origin of many such agencies in self-help/mutual-aid support groups—at a time when the disease was erroneously believed to be a "homosexual" one, illustrates several points made by Kahn. He notes that innovative programs are often provided by voluntary agencies prior to the development of a consensus about public responsibility for that particular program or client group. And while the general public is, on the one hand, likely to encourage innovation to provide services with increasing cost effectiveness, it is generally not willing to support population groups or activities that deviate widely from accepted social norms (Kahn, 1984). Stoesz also addresses this issue, when he talks about "marginal interest groups" (blacks, women, native Americans, homosexuals, Hispanics, rural residents) who have been neglected, excluded or oppressed by mainstream society. He states that in American culture, such groups are expected to gather resources and identify leadership to mount programs which serve the particular marginal group. Their success may be limited by financial restraints or the community may be unresponsive to groups that violate traditional norms—leaving them to fend for themselves (Stoesz, 1989).

So much care for persons-with-AIDS is currently being delivered on a community level that a special conference on conducting research in this area was convened in 1989 by the federal government's Agency for

Health Care Policy and Research. Almost twenty research reports were presented, dealing with such researchable issues as: home care, impact of caregiving on caregivers, use of paraprofessionals, availability of community services, ethical issues, and planning for continuous care (U.S. Department of Health and Human Services, 1990).

The AIDS crisis has now spread beyond the communities and groups originally identified as having high incidence/prevalence. As it has spread, the government and health professionals—in contrast to the initial heavy voluntary involvement—are taking more active roles in the control, treatment, prevention, and management of the disease (Harris County Medical Society, 1988; U.S. General Accounting Office, September 1988; Dunham, 1988; Dunham, 1989; Association of University Programs in Health Administration, 1990). A variety of clinical issues are being addressed (Blanchet, 1988; LeVee, 1989; Sechrest et al., 1989), as are legal and ethical issues (Dalton and Burris, 1987; Ryan and Rowe, 1988). Groups considered particularly vulnerable, such as college students, are receiving particular attention (Keeling, 1989; Richie et al., 1990). One expects that as this crisis permeates all races, economic groups, and subcultures, governmental involvement (at all levels) will increase, and treatment facilities will become more bureaucratic, and less community-based. Once effective agents for prevention and/or treatment are discovered and approved, the private sector will likely play a greater role on a proprietary basis. Already, the charge has been made that the combined efforts of the National Institutes of Health and one particular pharmaceutical company have led to a monopoly of AZT in the treatment of the disease (Nussbaum, 1990).

Domestic Assault Shelters

There is much disagreement over the definition of family or domestic violence (Emery, 1989). In its narrowest sense, "domestic violence" has been defined as the "use of physical force by one adult member of the household against another adult member" (Martin, 1987, p. 3). On a broader scale, the term "family violence" also encompasses physical force against children and the elderly, by others within the family unit (Bopp and Vardalis, 1989).

The battered women's movement began to evolve in the United States early in the 1970s (Pagelow, 1984). While wife battering was not new, and seems to date back to the beginning of monogamy at least (Martin, 1976), it did not gain attention until this time (Walker, 1979). Much of this attention must be attributed to the work of the women's liberation movement (Okun, 1986) and the creation of an environment conducive to finally examining this social problem.

In order to fully appreciate the evolution of domestic assault shelters to temporarily house persons who are the victims of domestic assault, it is necessary to place their development within the broader context of the Women's Movement in general, and the Women's Consumer Movement, in particular.

The feminist movement, in the last several decades, has called attention to the male domination of historical, societal, political, and economic events. In an attempt to give full credit to womens' roles in history (Sochen, 1974), it has unearthed considerable evidence that society's view toward women has traditionally been an ambiguous one, and this ambiguity especially reveals itself when a woman is a victim of assault (Deckard, 1975).

When a woman comes forth and identifies herself as such a victim, she becomes entangled with the legal, public safety and medical communities. Traditional attitudes that give men patriarchal authority to abuse their wives, can be found in the roots of legal systems, attitudes of judges, attitudes of male-dominated police forces, and of the male-dominated medical professions. These attitudes can be used to "rationalize" such male behavior (Sandelowski, 1981). On a broader scale, Gelles defines the problem as one of "selective inattention"—whereby our society has become so desensitized to all the violence around us that we are not able to perceive how the norm of violence was established and by which institutions it is generated and transmitted (Gelles, 1974).

As the feminist movement focused on issues of concern to women, the role of women as *consumers* of a variety of services received special attention. One of the most high-profile consumer marketplaces examined was that of health care (Boston Women's Health Book Collective, 1976; Turshen, 1989). Women requesting health care have often sought treatment for domestic assault. Estimates of the extent of wife battering often differ, because of lack of uniformity in the definition of the term "abuse" and the multiple obstacles presented in gathering this type of data (Pagelow, 1984). Estimates on the extent of battering among couples have ranged from a low of 21 percent (Russell, 1982) to a high of 35 percent (Frieze, 1980). While Strauss, Gelles, and Steinmetz's national survey documented a 28 percent incidence of battering, they estimated the "true" rate to be closer to 50 percent or 60 percent, with only 28 percent of couples admitting to battering (Strauss et al., 1980). These data seem to underscore the fact that women abuse is a problem of serious proportions.

This is not a new phenomenon, and in the United States, such records go back as far as the 1830s. Because public opinion has supported traditional male authority in the family, the problem has persisted and is found in all social/economic classes. Added to this problem are recent estimates that over 20 percent of children suffer physical abuse in the U.S., and reports of 500,000-to-one million annual cases of elderly abuse (Bopp and Vardalis, 1987, pp. 29–44). Some research also indicates that abuse of males by spouses might be much more prevalent than previously believed. The number of battered males is believed to be underestimated because of an embarrassed reluctance on the part of men to admit to such abuse, or seek help from authorities. Also, some are believed to stay in the abusive relationship in order to protect their children from maternal abuse, in a society where they fear custody laws following a breakup will favor placement of children with the mother (McNeely and Robinson-Simpson, 1987).

In the past decade, there has been a dramatic increase in the scope and magnitude of research into family violence (Van Hasselt et al., 1988). Some of this research has focused upon the different treatment modalities which have been tried, including: hospital emergency room intervention/detection/treatment; conjoint therapy; group therapy; the use of crisis intervention teams; focused intervention with the abusive partner; police intervention; treatment by family service agencies; and attempts to develop psychometric screening inventories to predict which women are at risk of abuse (Roberts, 1984; Lewis, 1985).

Other research has attempted to evaluate some of the programs which have been established, such as the study of a center for sexual assault victims (Ruch and Chandler, 1980). In addition, considerable attention has been focused in research on the concept of "blaming the victim" (Ryan, 1976)—wherein victims of abuse are treated in patronizing, accusatory, nonsympathetic ways, as if they "caused" the problem and "deserved" the assault. Sandelowski identifies this process as occurring in an "exceptionalistic" framework, where the behaviors of the batterer and/or victim are explained as due to exceptional deviance on the part of one or the other—rather than as due to the "root cause", which she sees as society's long-standing acceptance of sexism (Sandelowski, 1981).

Special attention has therefore been given to professionals who encounter victims of assault, such as police and medical personnel, in an attempt to identify those attitudes and psychological characteristics which are strong predictors of victim-blaming (Alexander, 1980).

In regard to the police, special attention has been paid to developing strong cooperative efforts between them and social workers, in order to prevent domestic abuse, make it easier for police to identify at-risk persons and refer them to the proper social agencies, and afford opportunities for social workers to organize seminars to educate police about the dynamics of domestic violence—all in an effort to promote early intervention (Abel and Suh, 1987). On the legislative level, police can play a more direct role in the area of domestic assault if state laws and police policies are changed. One experiment, based on a change in Minnesota state law and a subsequent related change in Minneapolis police policy, made it possible for police to make "probable cause" arrests, without a signed complaint from the victim. Arrest powers, used in this manner, appeared to be quite effective in reducing domestic violence in Minneapolis, although the researchers caution against widespread generalization of the findings (Sherman and Berk, 1984a).

In regard to medical personnel, it has been suggested that hospital emergency rooms develop and apply protocols to identify the battered woman—who comes for treatment of one type or another—in a manner similar to those used widely to identify child abuse (McLeer and Anwar, 1989). And, special attention needs to be paid to the *pregnant* woman, even when she comes for routine prenatal care, including examination for hypertension, diabetes, malnutrition, etc. A random study of pregnant women seeking routine prenatal care from both public and private clinics revealed a distressful number who had been battered during pregnancy. The best predictor for such abuse was *prior* abuse (before the pregnancy). In view of the additional potential complications of spontaneous abortions or stillbirths as a result of such beatings, the researchers recommended that prenatal care should include assessment of the woman's physical *safety*, as well. In addition to the physical danger to both mother and fetus, some battered pregnant women may turn to drug-alcohol use to cope with their predicament, only adding to the negative consequences (Helton et al., 1987).

Research in the area of domestic assault, in addition to identifying it as an *international* problem, and not one confined to the United States (Gelles and Connell, 1983), has consistently emphasized the importance of the absence of a support network in the dynamics of the problem. Often, the abusive family is found to lack meaningful associations outside the home (Neidig and Friedman, 1984).

A variety of services (including emergency shelters, hotlines, and counseling) has evolved—often from grassroots feminist activity, to provide outside support to such families—from feminist organizations, social service agencies, and community mental health centers. The medical community and public safety departments have also improved the training of staff in hospital emergency rooms and special police assault units (Bopp and Vardalis, 1987).

Domestic assault shelters, often anonymously located in ordinary-looking homes in residential neighborhoods (for security purposes), are therefore but one part of a larger societal attempt to deal with family violence in general. Similar to the modern hospice movement, the current shelter movement is acknowledged to have begun in England in 1970. At that time, a group of women in a London neighborhood began to meet to protest high food costs, and gradually discovered other mutual concerns. They eventually leased a condemned house from the government, to enable them to expand their gathering and dispensing of information on legal and welfare rights (Pagelow, 1984). Shortly after Chiswick's Women's Aid opened its doors in 1971, women and their children began to seek overnight refuge from their violent spouses and the shelter movement was established (Dobash and Dobash, 1979). In 1974, Erin Pizzey, one of the founders of Chiswick's Women's Aid, published a book about the daily lives of battered women (*Scream Quietly or the Neighbours Will Hear*), which helped obtain international media attention for the battered women's movement (Pizzey, 1974).

Shortly thereafter, in the United States, feminist and grassroots groups began to become involved in both research and the delivery of services to women who were battered (Pagelow, 1984). The first shelter established exclusively for battered women was probably Women's House in St. Paul, Minnesota, which started as a phone service in 1972 and opened as a shelter in 1974 (Martin, 1976). Between 1974 and 1983, the number of women's shelters multiplied rapidly, to more than 600 shelters (Okun, 1986). And during his presidency (1976–1980), Jimmy Carter established the Office of Domestic Violence in the Department of Health and Human Services—the main purpose of which was to coordinate federal efforts in providing services to victimized family members (Roberts, 1981, p. vii).

The first nationwide survey of domestic assault shelters was conducted by Roberts in 1978. Eighty-nine such shelters responded to the survey. The majority had been funded in the late 1970s. About half were located in separate, free-standing facilities. About 20 percent were located in private homes, and another 20 percent were at the YWCA. Admissions criteria included the presence of violence or threats—including abuse to children. Persons with drug/alcohol problems, communicable diseases, or recently-released from prison, were generally excluded. The agencies were voluntary, not-for-profit, and attempted to keep their locations secret, for security purposes. The most commonly-offered services included: emergency telephone services; 24-hour intervention; individual counseling; welfare/legal/court advocacy; support/caring; transportation to shelter; vocational training; mediation program for abusers; shelter; child advocacy; interagency and community reporting/ referral services; coordination with criminal justice agencies; and training of volunteers. The staff tended to be mostly volunteers, plus paid CETA (Comprehensive Employment Training Act) employees. Board members were likely to be lawyers, social workers, formerly battered women, mental health professionals, teachers, and nurses. Funding sources included grants from private foundations, the federal government (CETA, the Law Enforcement Assistance Administration); state funds; local mental health associations; and community donations (Roberts, 1981).

Most women's shelters today offer a variety of services for the battered women which are not found elsewhere within the social service system, and which are generally offered with a better understanding of the woman as victim. Aid To Victims of Domestic Assault (AVDA), a shelter in Florida, upon whose founding board one of the authors of this book once sat, offers the following services, which appear to be typical of shelter programs nationwide:

24-hour crisis hotline
shelter for battered women and their children
crisis intervention services
direct services and counseling
court assistance
family information and referral services
information speakers bureau
comprehensive training for all program volunteers
criminal justice training

While the growth in the number of shelters in the last decade may be considered as one measure of the essential nature of the community service they provide, the reported high percentage (over 40%) of women who return to their battering partners after a shelter stay has vexed both shelter staff and researchers during this same time frame (Aguirre, 1985, p. 352). While some have been discouraged by this high return rate, it may also be viewed as an indicator of new directions in the shelter movement. Davis, in her article tracing changes in perspectives on the problem, discusses "decreased attention to women" and "increased attention to men" (Davis, 1987, p. 309). The latter is already evident in the increased focus on the treatment of batterers (DeMaris and Jackson, 1987; Star, 1983) and support for criminal justice reforms across the United States (Sherman and Berk, 1984b). As to the former, rather than "decreased attention," perhaps a somewhat different perspective may be more useful. The data from a survey of residents in 15 shelters in Texas found that the "only statistically significant predictor is the respondent's source of income. . . . the probability of wives returning to abusive husbands increases considerably if their husbands are their sole source of support" (Aguirre, 1985, p. 352). It therefore appears that while domestic assault shelters are important alternative resources for battered women, their ultimate efficacy has been questioned by those who see such attempts as largely palliative until widespread education on the causes and eradication of sexism can be instituted (Sandelowski, 1981). The return rate also underscores the need for social service providers to focus their prevention and intervention efforts on the family as a whole, which is often acknowledged as a goal when appropriate resources are available.

In the meantime, Marieskind has identified two major forms of activism to improve the health of women (including those who are physically and emotionally abused): (1) supplementing the status quo with a much-needed service; and (2) providing alternative processes within traditional structures. To the extent that domestic assault shelters provide the only feasible place of safe-harbor for some isolated victims of abuse during especially dangerous periods, they can serve as an example of the former. And to the extent that the separation they provide can "force" alternative therapeutic processes upon both the abuser and victim in some instances, they can also serve as an example of the latter. Marieskind believes that even though such shelters often do not create basic changes simply because of their existence, the palliative safety valve they can provide is a *vital* service, along with others (Marieskind, 1980).

THE EVOLUTION OF NEW HSOs

Some years ago, Arthur Stinchcombe called attention to the precarious nature of new organizations, referring to the "liability of newness"— the greater likelihood of a young organization to fail, in comparison to an older, established one. He postulated that this liability occurs because the management and staff of young organizations have to learn new roles—and simultaneously deal with problems of socialization, coordination, productivity, etc. (Stinchcombe, 1965).

Building on Stinchcombe's analysis, Wiewel and Hunter identified three processes which can aid in the survival of new organizations: resource exchange, legitimation, and domain definition. The resources necessary for functioning can come from a variety of sources, including similar organizations which are cooperative (not competitive) with the new organization. In some instances, the new organization may actually be a spin-off of, or addition to, an existing organization. Legitimation is necessary to give the organization and its activities the authority and respect needed in order to attract confident clients. And domain definition addresses the importance of determining what to do, for whom, where and why—and applying the aforementioned acquired resources and legitimation to those activities (Wiewel and Hunter, 1985).

In applying Stinchcombe's "liability of newness" concept to voluntary social service organizations in particular, Singh et al., found the *external legitimacy* variable to be more predictive of longevity than another— that of *internal coordination*. Legitimation variables, such as licensing, accreditation, size, and composition of the board of directors, and professional association recognition, may be more positively associated with survival of new organizations than internal organizational changes that attempt to improve internal coordination (Singh et al., 1986).

At this point, the four types of new HSOs discussed above appear to be surviving in general, although there likely have been individual agency failures, reorganizations, mergers. All four types have certainly achieved legitimacy, both with the public and with human service professionals.

In addition to organizational *survival*, the question of organizational *evolution* is also of interest (Greiner, 1972). When one reviews the above discussion of four new HSOs which came into prominence in the past several decades (hospices, continuing/life care, AIDS services agencies, and domestic assault shelters) there appear to be some common evolutionary stages among them, as follows:

Stage 1:   In this stage, the problem is perceived as largely existing on an individual level—with persons often not aware of the fact that many others are experiencing the same problem and are equally frustrated by the lack of an institutional solution. Thus, terminally-ill persons die "alone," often without the host of psychological, social, economic, spiritual and physical comforts required during the dying process; elderly live in fear of confusing, unsafe and unstable surroundings; Persons-with-AIDS endure all the physical, social, economic, and legal consequences of the disease—with little or no support; and battered spouses stay with their mates and try to keep the abuse they receive a secret from neighbors and authorities.

Stage 2:   In this stage, persons with the problem, or concerned about the problem because a relative or friend is directly involved, begin to speak out and identify themselves. The problem gains a higher profile. Its scope begins to impinge on the public consciousness. As persons come forward, identified with the problem, it assumes a human face. The problem begins to be addressed by radio and television talk-show hosts, and newspaper and magazine columnists/writers. Gradually, the problems of the dying, elderly, Persons-with-AIDS, and victims of domestic assault are no longer hidden, or considered in "bad taste" to discuss openly.

Stage 3:   In this stage, pioneering efforts slowly evolve—sometimes, but not always, led by an individual, or small coterie, to address the issue on a limited basis. Thus, Dame Cicely Saunders establishes the first modern hospice in London; fraternal/religious groups—concerned about their elderly members—establish continuing/life care centers; Persons-with-AIDS form support groups to help each other, which later evolve into agencies offering a variety of services, provided in part by volunteers who are HIV-free; and women's organizations—such as the YWCA and feminist groups—provide shelters for abused women and their children.

Stage 4:   By this stage, a body of literature, research reports, and statistical data have developed to form a critical mass, giving scientific underpining to the claims of the concerned individuals and groups who have carried the torch to date. Thus, the "death and dying" literature of Kubler-Ross, and others, emerges to be incorporated into the hospice movement; demographics on the elderly, and research into gerontology, add insight into the spectrum of elderly concerns addressed by the continuing/life care model; epidemiological data on AIDS more clearly suggest the vectors through which the disease most likely travels, and its increasing spread to groups other than those initially associated with it. These data also have implications for prevention, and possible treatment and/or cure; statistics from police and medical reports, as well as theories on the origin, prevention, and treatment of domestic assault, are available to be used in concert—to attempt to provide solutions to this problem (one such solution, no matter how temporary, being the assault shelter).

Stage 5: By the time this stage has been reached, the aforementioned forces have brought the problem to the attention of government, via the media and through lobbying efforts of concerned individuals and groups— the latter of which may now have statewide or national volunteer/ professional coalitions (American Association of Retired Persons, National Hospice Organization, etc.). The pressure brought to bear results in administrative/legislative attempts to deal with at least a part of the problem. Thus, the argument that hospice care is likely to be less expensive than traditional inpatient hospital care for the terminally ill, leads to the passage of an amendment to the Social Security Act, allowing Medicare reimbursement for hospice care; presidents convene White House Conferences on Aging, and a variety of laws are passed addressing elderly needs for health care, housing, etc.; governmental attempts to conduct AIDS research are dramatically increased and the Food and Drug Administration accelerates the review process for new drugs to treat AIDS, so that AZT, for example, is made available more quickly than is usual in the case of experimental or untried drugs; and in the domestic assault arena, laws are passed in the states, giving the police more powers of arrest and judges more treatment options for offenders— and President Carter creates the Office of Domestic Violence, bringing heightened awareness to the public.

Figure 2 contains a summary of this evolutionary process. While there may well be variations from this model, when one takes a closer look at these four, and other, "new" HSOs, the general outline appears to the authors of this volume to be a "reasonable fit" upon which to base further discussion. The extent to which new HSOs, which emerge in the next decade or so, will follow this process remains to be seen. Speculation on that matter will be addressed in Part IV.

FIGURE 2 THE EVOLUTION OF NEW HUMAN SERVICES ORGANIZATIONS

Stage 1
The "problem" is viewed here as an individual one and remains "low profile." There is an absence of systematic, organizational solutions.

Stage 2
The problem becomes more visible and receives media attention, as persons concerned with the problem become more vocal and active in addressing it.

Stage 3
Pioneering solutions, often on an individual or local basis, are attempted in order to address the problem. These efforts are overwhelmingly of a voluntary, not-for-profit nature.

Stage 4
Statistical data, research findings, and theoretical literature accumulate to guide lay, professional and governmental resources in addressing the problem.

Stage 5
Through legislative and administrative policy decisions, government, at the federal and/or state levels, takes action to address the problem. By now, citizen organizations have emerged to provide intense lobbying on aspects of the problem of particular concern to them.

REFERENCES

Abel, Eileen Mazur and Edward K. Suh. "Use of Police Services by Battered Women," *Social Work*, Vol. 32, No. 6, November–December 1987, pp. 526–528.

Aguirre, B.E. "Why Do They Return? Abused Wives in Shelters," *Social Work*, Vol. 30, No. 4, July–August 1985, pp. 350–354.

Alexander, Cheryl. "Blaming the Victim: A Comparison of Police and Nurses' Perceptions of Victims of Rape," *Women and Health*, Vol. 5, No. 1, Spring 1980, pp. 65–79.

Alperin, Diane and Nicholas Richie. "Social Services in Continuing/Life Care Communities: Implications for Social Work Education," *Arete*, Vol. 13, No. 1, Summer 1988, pp. 29–34.

Alperin, Diane and Nicholas Richie. "Community-Based AIDS Service Organizations:

Challenges and Educational Preparation," *Health and Social Work*, Vol. 14, No. 3, 1989, pp. 165–173.

Alperin, Diane and Nicholas Richie. "Continuing/Life Care Facilities and the Continuum of Care," *Journal of Housing for the Elderly*, Vol. 6, Nos. 1/2, 1990, pp. 125–130. Also published in *Aging in Place*, Leon Pastalan, (ed.). Binghamton: Haworth Press, 1990, pp. 125–130.

Association of University Programs in Health Administration. *HIV/AIDS Training Institute for Administrators of Health Care Organizations: AIDS Management Issues for Senior Administrators*. Ft. Myers, VA: AUPHA, March 1990.

Atherton, Charles. "Liberalism's Decline and the Threat to the Welfare State," *Social Work*, Vol. 35, No. 2, March 1990, pp. 163–167.

Bell, D. *The Coming of the Post-Industrial Society: A Venture in Social Forecasting.* New York: Basic Books, 1973.

Blanchet, Kevin. *AIDS: A Health Care Management Response.* Rockville, MD: Aspen, 1988.

Bopp, William and James Vardalis. *Crimes Against Women.* Springfield, IL: Charles C Thomas, 1987.

Boston Women's Health Book Collective. *Our Bodies, Ourselves.* New York: Simon and Schuster, 1976.

Brager, George and Stephen Holloway. *Changing Human Service Organizations.* New York: Free Press, 1978.

Buckingham, Robert. *The Complete Hospice Guide.* New York: Harper and Row, 1983.

Bureau of Economic and Business Research. *1988 Florida Statistical Abstract.* Gainesville, FL: The University Presses of Florida, 1988.

Butler, Robert. *Why Survive? Being Old in America.* New York: Harper and Row, 1975.

Centers for Disease Control. *HIV/AIDS Surveillance.* Washington, DC: USDH&HS, May 1991.

Centers for Disease Control. *HIV/AIDS Prevention Newsletter.* Vol. 1, No. 1, October 1990.

Cohen, Kenneth. *Hospice — Prescription for Terminal Care.* Germantown, MD: Aspen, 1979.

Curran, M. Stroud. "Lifetime Promises to Residents: Can They Be Kept?" *Lifecare Industry.* Philadelphia: Laventhol and Horwath, 1983, pp. 6–8.

Dalton, Harlon and Scott Burris, (eds.). *AIDS and the Law.* New Haven: Yale University Press, 1987.

Davis, Liane. "Battered Women: The Transformation of a Social Problem," *Social Work*, Vol. 32, No. 4, July–August 1987, pp. 306–311.

Day, Phyllis J. "The New Poor in America: Isolationism in an International Political Economy," *Social Work*, Vol. 34, No. 3, May 1989, pp. 227–233.

Deckard, Barbara. *The Women's Movement.* New York: Harper and Row, 1975.

Demaris, A. and J. Jackson. "Batterers' Reports of Recidivism After Counseling," *Social Casework*, Vol. 68, No. 8, 1987, pp. 458–465.

Dobash, R. Emerson and Russell P. Dobash. *Violence Against Wives: A Case Against the Patriarchy.* New York: Free Press, 1979.

Drucker, Peter. *The New Realities.* New York: Harper and Row, 1989.

Dunham, Nancy. *Task Force Report on HIV/AIDS and Health Services Administration Education.* Rockville, MD: Bureau of Health Professions, PHS, DHHS, January, 1988.

Dunham, Nancy. "Promoting Effective Managerial Responses to the AIDS Epidemic: The Task Force on AIDS and Health Services Administration Education," *Journal of Health Administration Education,* Vol. 7, No. 1, Winter 1989, pp. 113–121.

Emery, Robert E. "Family Violence," *American Psychologist,* Vol. 44, No. 2, February 1989, pp. 321–328.

Everglades Area Health Education Center. *Images and Insights—Facing Death from the Arts and Popular Culture.* West Palm Beach, FL: Everglades AHEC, February 3, 1989.

Ford Foundation Project on Social Welfare and the American Future. *The Common Good: Social Welfare and the American Future.* New York: Ford Foundation, May 1989.

Frieze, Irene. "Causes and Consequences of Marital Rape," Paper presented at the Annual Meeting of the American Psychological Association, Montreal, Canada, 1980.

Gelles, Richard. *The Violent Home.* Beverly Hills, CA: Sage Publications, 1974.

Gelles, Richard and Claire P. Connell. *International Perspectives on Family Violence.* Lexington, MA: Lexington Books, 1983.

Gottlieb, M.S. et al. "Pneumoceptis Carinii Pneumonia and Mucosal Candidiasis in Previously Healthy Homosexual Men: Evidence of a New Acquired Cellular Immunodeficiency," *New England Journal of Medicine,* Vol. 305, 1981, pp. 1425–1431.

Greiner, Larry. "Evolution and Revolution as Organizations Grow," *Harvard Business Review,* July–August 1972, Vol. 50, pp. 37–46.

Gulick, Gary. *Independent Retirement Living: The Story of Life Care Retirement.* Des Moines, IA: Life Care Services Corporation, 1979.

Hamilton, Michael and Helen Reid, (eds.). *A Hospice Handbook: A New Way to Care for the Dying.* Grand Rapids: William Eerdmans, 1980.

Harrington, Michael. *The Other America: Poverty in the United States.* New York: Macmillan, 1962.

Harris County Medical Society. *AIDS: A Guide for Survival.* Houston: Harris County Medical Society and Houston Academy of Medicine, 1988.

Harrison, Mary and Nicholas Richie. "The First Decade: A Hospice Case Study," *The American Journal of Hospice Care,* Vol. 5, No. 6, November/December 1988, pp. 43–47.

Hartman, Ann. "Our Global Village," *Social Work,* Vol. 35, No. 4, July 1990, pp. 291–292.

Helton, Anne Stewart et al. "Battered and Pregnant: A Prevalence Study," *American Journal of Public Health,* Vol. 77, No. 10, October 1987, pp. 1337–1339.

Kahn, Ernest. "The Voluntary Sector Can Remain Alive—and Well," in *Human Services at Risk,* Felice Perlmutter, (ed.)., Lexington, MA: Lexington Books, 1984, Ch. 4, pp. 57–74.

Keeling, Richard, (ed.). *AIDS on the College Campus*. Rockville, MD: American College Health Association, 1989.

Kohlert, Nancy. "Welfare Reform: A Historic Consensus," *Social Work*, Vol. 34, No. 4, July 1989, pp. 303–306.

Kubler-Ross, Elisabeth. *On Death and Dying*. New York: Macmillan, 1970.

LeVee, William, (ed.). *New Perspectives on HIV-Related Illnesses: Progress in Health Services Research*. NCHSR & HCTA, PHS, USDH&HS, Washington, DC: Government Printing Office, September 1989.

Lewis, Bonnie Yegidis. "The Wife Abuse Inventory: A Screening Device for the Identification of Abused Women," *Social Work*, Vol. 30, No. 1, January–February 1985, pp. 32–35.

Lewis, Oscar. *Five Families*. New York: Basic Books, 1959.

Macarov, David. *Certain Change: Social Work Practice in the Future*. Silver Spring, MD: National Association of Social Workers, 1991.

Marieskind, Helen. *Women in the Health System*. St. Louis, MO: C.V. Mosby, 1980.

Martin, Del. *Battered Wives*. New York: Pocket Books, 1976.

Martin, Del. "The Historical Roots of Domestic Violence," in *Domestic Violence on Trial*, Daniel Sonkin, (ed.). New York: Springer, 1987, Chapter 1, pp. 3.20.

Maslow, Abraham. *Motivation and Personality*. New York: Harper and Row, 1970.

McLeer, Susan and Rebecca Anwar. "A Study of Battered Women Presenting in an Emergency Department," *American Journal of Public Health*, Vol. 79, No. 1, January 1989, pp. 65–66.

McNearney, Walter. "The Role of Technology in the Development of Health Institutional Goals and Programs," in *Technology and Health Care Systems in the 1980s*, Morris Collen (ed.). Washington, DC: USDHEW, January 1972, pp. 101–112.

McNeely, R.L. and Gloria Robinson-Simpson. "The Truth About Domestic Violence: A Falsely Framed Issue," *Social Work*, Vol. 32, No. 6, November–December 1987, pp. 485–490.

Mumford, Lewis. *The Myth of the Machine — Volume I: Techniques and Human Development*. New York: Harcourt, Brace, World, 1967.

Mumford, Lewis. *The Myth of the Machine — Volume II: The Pentagon of Power*. New York: Harcourt, Brace, Jovanovich, 1970.

Murray, Charles. *Losing Ground — American Social Policy: 1950-1980*. New York: Basic Books, 1984.

Naisbitt, John. *Megatrends: Ten New Directions for Transforming Our Lives*. New York: Warner Books, 1982.

Naisbitt, John and Patricia Aburdene. *Megatrends 2000: Ten New Directions for the 1990s*. New York: William Morrow, 1990.

National Hospice Organization. *Locator Directory of Hospices in America: 1990*. McLean, VA: NHO, 1990.

Neidig, Peter and Dale Friedman. *Spouse Abuse*. Champaign, IL: Research Press, 1984.

Nussbaum, Bruce. *Good Intentions: How Big Business and the Medical Establishment Are Corrupting the Fight Against Aids*. Boston: Atlantic Monthly Press, 1990.

Okun, Lewis. *Woman Abuse*. Albany: State University of New York Press, 1986.

Pagelow, Mildred. *Family Violence.* New York: Praeger, 1984.

Perlmutter, Felice. "A Theoretical Model of Social Agency Development," *Social Casework,* October 1969, pp. 467–473.

Pizzey, Erin. *Scream Quietly or the Neighbours Will Hear.* Short Hills: Ridley Enslow, 1974.

Raper, Ann Trueblood. *National Continuing Care Directory.* Glenview, IL: Scott Foresman, 1984.

Reischauer, R. "America's Underclass," *Public Welfare,* Vol. 45, No. 4, 1987, pp. 26–31.

Richie, Nicholas D. "An Approach to Hospice Program Evaluation", *The American Journal of Hospice Care.* Vol. 4, No. 5, September/October 1987, pp. 20–27.

Richie, Nicholas D., Doris Stenroos, and Adelaide Getty. "Using Peer Educators for a Classroom-Based AIDS Program," *Journal of American College Health,* Vol. 39, No. 2, September 1990, pp. 96–99.

Roberts, Albert. *Sheltering Battered Women: A National Study and Service Guide.* New York: Springer, 1981.

Roberts, Albert (ed.). *Battered Women and their Families.* New York: Springer, 1984.

Rose, A. "Continuing Care Retirement Centers: An Expansion Opportunity," *American Health Care Association Journal,* Vol. 9, No. 3, 1983.

Ruch, Libby O. and Susan M. Chandler. "An Evaluation of a Center for Sexual Assault Victims," *Women and Health,* Vol. 5, No. 1, Spring 1980, pp. 45–63.

Russell, Diana. *Rape in Marriage.* New York: Macmillan, 1982.

Ryan, W. *Blaming the Victim.* New York: Vintage Books, 1976.

Ryan, C. and M. Rowe. "AIDS: Legal and Ethical Issues," *Social Casework,* Vol. 69, 1988, pp. 324–333.

Sandelowski, Margaret. *Women, Health and Choice.* Englewood Cliffs, NJ: Prentice-Hall, 1981.

Schwab, Teresa, (ed.). *Caring for An Aging World: International Models for Long Term Care, Financing and Delivery.* New York: McGraw-Hill, 1989.

Sechrest, Lee, Howard Freeman, and Albert Mulley, (eds.). *Health Services Research Methodology: A Focus on AIDS.* NCHSR & HCTA, PHS, USDH & HS, Washington, DC: Government Printing Office, September 1989.

Sherman, Lawrence and Richard Berk. "The Minneapolis Domestic Violence Experiment," *Police Foundation Reports.* Washington, DC: Police Foundation, April 1984a.

Sherman, Lawrence and Richard Berk. "The Specific Deterrent Effects of Arrest for Domestic Assault," *American Sociological Review,* Vol. 49, April 1984b, pp. 261–272.

Shilts, Randy. *And the Band Played On — Politics, People and the AIDS Epidemic.* New York: Penguin Books, 1988.

Singh, Jitendra, Donald Tucker and Robert House. "Organizational Legitimacy and the Liability of Newness," *Administrative Science Quarterly,* Vol. 31, 1986, pp. 171–193.

Sochen, June. *Herstory.* New York: Alfred, 1974.

Star, Barbara. *Helping the Abuser.* New York: Family Service Association of America, 1983.

Steinhauer, Marcia B. "Innovation and Change in Organizations: The Absorbing and Sustaining of New Attributes," in *Handbook of Human Services Administration,*

Jack Rabin and Marcia B. Steinhauer, (eds.). New York: Marcel Dekker, 1988, Ch. 13, pp. 445–473.

Stern, Mark. "The Politics of American Social Welfare," in *Human Services at Risk,* Felice Perlmutter, (ed.). Lexington, MA: Lexington Books, 1984, Ch. 1, pp. 3–21.

Stinchcombe, Arthur L. "Social Structures and Organizations," in *Handbook of Organizations,* James G. March, (ed.). Chicago: Rand McNally, 1965, pp. 142–193.

Stoesz, David. "A Theory of Social Welfare," *Social Work,* Vol. 34, No. 2, 1989, pp. 101–107.

Stoesz, David and Howard Jacob Karger. "Welfare Reform: From Illusion to Reality," *Social Work,* Vol. 35, No. 2, March 1990, pp. 141–147.

Straus, Murray, Richard Gelles, and Suzanne Steinmetz. *Behind Closed Doors: Violence in the American Family.* New York: Doubleday, 1980.

Toffler, Alvin. *Powershift.* New York: Bantam Books, 1990.

Torrens, Paul, (ed.). *Hospice Programs and Public Policy.* Chicago: American Hospital Association, 1985.

Towle, Charlotte. *Common Human Needs.* New York: National Association of Social Workers, 1965.

Turshen, Meredith. "Women's Health," in *The Politics of Public Health,* New Brunswick, NJ: Rutgers University Press, 1989, Chapter 5, pp. 91–118.

U.S. Department of Commerce. Bureau of the Census, *Statistical Abstract of the United States 1990.* Washington, DC: Government Printing Office, 1990.

U.S. Department of Health and Human Services. *Community-Based Care of Persons with AIDS: Developing a Research Agenda.* Washington, DC: Government Printing Office, April 1990.

United States General Accounting Office. *AIDS Education: Reaching Populations at Higher Risk.* Washington, DC: Government Printing Office, September 1988.

Van Hasselt, Vincent et al. (eds.). *Handbook of Family Violence.* New York: Plenum Press, 1988.

Walker, Lenore. *The Battered Woman.* New York: Harper Colophon, 1979.

Wiewel, Wim and Albert Hunter. "The Interorganizational Network as a Resource: A Comparative Case Study on Organizational Genesis," *Administrative Science Quarterly,* Vol. 30, 1985, pp. 482–496.

Wilson, William. *The Truly Disadvantaged.* Chicago: University of Chicago Press, 1990.

World Health Organization. "WHO Predicts Up to 30 Million World AIDS Cases by Year 2000," *The Nation's Health,* Washington, DC: American Public Health Association, January 1991, p. 1.

PART III

THE HUMAN SERVICES WORKER—A PROPOSAL

CLIENT DISSATISFACTION WITH THE HUMAN SERVICES

As indicated in Part I of this volume, the federal government became involved in some areas of concern to consumers early in the twentieth century. Those concerns encompassed unsafe medical products/ services, included in the definition of "human services" upon which this volume is based. Over the ensuing decades, more and more regulatory agencies were added on the federal level to protect consumers—the Food and Drug Administration, Federal Aviation Administration, Environmental Protection Agency, among others (Jones and Gardner, 1976). Related regulatory agencies were often established by various states (Maloney, 1976). Today, these agencies are often attacked for ineffectiveness, due to alleged collusion with the industries they are charged to regulate, via the interworkings of the "regulatory-industrial complex" (Nader, 1973).

The "consumer movement," as we know it today, essentially emerged in its current form during the 1960s. Individuals and groups—such as the Consumers Union, have increasingly demanded that the marketplace be made more responsive to the needs and concerns of consumers. And as they have become better educated, consumers have been prone to make their dissatisfaction known and to devote time and resources to "the movement" (Landsman, 1976).

A variety of forces appear to play a part in the consumer movement, as presently constituted. While persons from different social classes see the world (and marketplace) somewhat differently (Mott, 1978; Clode et al., 1987), a fundamental problem is seen to be the growth of "megastructures" (big government, big business, big labor, big bureaucracies) which can lead to a corresponding diminution in the value of the individual. Thus, attempts in recent years to "empower" consumers have included the use of "mediating structures"—such as neighborhoods, families, churches, and voluntary associations (Berger and Neuhaus, 1977).

Mitchell has pointed out that the information received by consumers, in the course of making their marketplace decisions, is a crucial variable, both in terms of its quantity *and* quality (Mitchell, 1978). And Spencer argues that technological advances have led to overexpectations on the part of consumers, and misunderstandings in their interactions with providers (Spencer, 1972).

When one examines the human services arena specifically, several classic works come to mind. For instance, the work of Hollingshead and Redlich illustrated, over three decades ago, that consumers of mental health services receive different diagnoses and treatment modalities, depending upon their social class (Hollingshead and Redlich, 1958). And Herbert Klarman initiated a new view of the health care marketplace when he argued that traditional economic analysis—which postulated an informed consumer, making rational decisions in a free-market setting—was inappropriate. Klarman pointed to the following idiosyncracies of the health care market, which limit traditional analysis of consumer behavior (Klarman, 1965):

1. The fact that health care is often of an emergent nature, and not a matter of choice and careful planning.

2. The fact that even when choice is technically available, the consumer may not be in a position (unconscious/unsophisticated) to exercise it.

3. The fact that physicians—as the "gatekeepers"—have traditionally made many of the choices *for* health care consumers (location of treatment/type of treatment, etc.).

4. The fact that "shopping around" was discouraged by professional societies, and sometimes by state laws, which severely limited provider competition through prohibitions on advertising, and other common marketing techniques.

5. The fact that "free entry" to the marketplace, on the part of providers, was extremely limited in most instances—due to educational/licensing/certification criteria.

6. The fact that "externalities" exist in health care, whereby the decision of one person to seek or not seek treatment (especially in the case of contagious disease) can affect another's well-being.

The Johnson Administration's War on Poverty, referred to in Part I, established the principle that human services agencies include representatives from the target population on their boards. These representatives were to be more than "window-dressing." They were to enjoy "maximum feasible participation," while at the same time representing the racial/ethnic/client populations served by the respective agencies (Rice, 1990). In addition, members of the target populations were sometimes hired as paid employees, who usually worked in the agency's "outreach" projects as liaisons between providers and consumers (Riley, 1981). In the most idealistic situation, empowered clients are encouraged to seek out resources, appeal unsatisfactory decisions, and join groups and coalitions aimed at changing policies and procedures which negatively affect their existence (Minahan, 1987, p. 592).

In the human services, the consumer movement has many manifestations. An overriding concern for many such agencies, and their clients, has been the "optimization of human functioning"—consistent with Maslow's principle of self-actualization, mentioned earlier (Schon, 1976; Maslow, 1970; Boyer, 1975). Human service consumers have also been concerned about unattractive/unsafe agency environments, lack of privacy, violations of confidentiality, inability to make informed treatment choices, stigmatizing policies and procedures, the feeling of second-class citizenship, bureaucratic hostility and red tape, and punitive control, among others (Huttman, 1981; Blumenstein, 1988).

The federal government has attempted to address the "product" side of consumerism (including *medical* products), via the establishment in 1972 of the National Consumer Product Safety Commission—an outgrowth of a study commission convened during the Johnson Administration. This agency places the responsibility for safe products upon their manufacturers (Pittle, 1976). And the not-for-profit Consumers Union continues to be concerned about a wide range of health-related products/services, including prescription drugs (brand name versus generic), new products/treatments, and the efficacy/cost/safety of products (Consumers Union, 1983). Indeed, specialized research is nowadays conducted on such human service consumer issues, among others, as: factors which account for patients' satisfaction with their physicians (Friedman and Churchill, 1987); consumer information necessary to make appropriate choices regarding health maintenance organization enrollment (Consumers Union, 1982; Zaltman and Sternthal, 1975, pp. 45–69); how to choose a qualified physician for a specific problem/client need (Consumers Health Services, 1989); and factors associated with consumption by families of mental health services (Zaltman and Sternthal, 1975, pp. 35–44).

Concern over the above, and related issues, has prompted various social and other not-for-profit agencies to employ consumer market strategies originally developed for the for-profit market, in an attempt to reach their target populations—both for the provision of services and the solicitation of funds (Loudon and Della Bitta, 1984). MacStravic, and others, have been careful to point out that the application of marketing strategies to the human services (health care, in particular) should be tempered by a desire to locate legitimate unmet consumer needs and provide information on how those needs can be satisfied—rather than to "sell" consumers products/services they *don't* really need (MacStravic, 1977).

Taken as a whole, consumer-related research in the human services has produced mixed results. As Breslow has pointed out, the alienated human services consumer is likely to be concerned with: the growing impersonality of service; lack of coordination of services; lack of comprehensive services; inequities based on race/ethnicity/social class; "irrational," unbending bureaucracies; and the very basic issue of the "right" to quality service (Breslow, 1972).

We shall now turn to a specific proposal which the authors of this volume believe is capable of alleviating *some* of the concerns of human services clients in communities where it can be implemented.

DESCRIPTION OF THE ROLE OF THE HUMAN SERVICES WORKER

Brager and Holloway have pointed out that social institutions are the products of the values and beliefs of the society in which they are located, and that in American society, there are conflicting ideologies with which human services agencies must contend. These include: societal ambivalence over the efficacy of institutionalized human services; a contradictory mandate from publicly-funded human service organizations—because of a fear of encouraging client dependency and/or client exploitation; and basic questions about the role of the provider, and his/her autonomy from control by the agency/employer (Brager and Holloway, 1978). To the extent that these, and related, conflicts exist, it is not surprising that clients have expressed the kinds of dissatisfaction discussed above. The situation for clients becomes especially confusing when one considers several other aspects of the human services delivery process—the profusion of staff in a single agency, and the frequent lack of coordination of services for individuals/families with multiple problems.

Austin has pointed out that in a single human service agency, the staff a client might encounter may include: paid, fully-trained professionals with degrees related to the primary purpose of the agency; paid, fully-trained professionals with degrees related to an ancillary purpose of the agency; paid staff who are not professionally trained in the human services; paid staff who are minimally trained as technicians in collaboration with professional staff, i.e., they are "paraprofessionals"; paid staff who perform support functions; and unpaid volunteers who provide various services (Austin, 1981, p. 87). Assuming such a variety of staff not only vary in their educational backgrounds but also, to some extent, in their values and attitudes toward the agency and its clients, the probability for confusion/disenchantment with services on the part of the client is likely to be enhanced.

Adding to the above problems is the fact that the human services "system" is variously defined and variously functional and effective, from one community to another. A common definition of a "system" is "a set of bounded, interacting parts that are coordinated in order to accomplish a goal" (Abels and Murphy, 1981, p. 48). When applying the systems approach to the human services, one also assumes that the "interacting parts" referred to in the definition represent a "holistic" view—in that they offer all the services needed to cope with the multifaceted nature of most human problems—including physical, psychological, economic, social, and other dimensions. When Abels and Murphy apply this perspective to the human services, they find a complex maze of conflicting and competing goals, agencies, and centers of power. The resultant confusion creates a host of difficulties for all concerned—including both clients and staff (Abels and Murphy, 1981, pp. 60–61).

When the above-mentioned deficiencies of, and dissatisfaction with, the human service system are considered in the light of the expected trends in the 1990s (discussed in Part II), there would appear to be severe financial, social, and political limits on drastic changes in the human services during the next decade. For this reason, the authors of this volume are suggesting a *modification*, through the introduction of a "new" human services professional, to be called the Human Services Worker (HSW). This proposal attempts to accomplish the following:

1. Preserve as much of the current human services structure as possible, because of the likelihood that additional funding will be in short supply in the 1990s.

2. Continue to recognize the legitimate human service roles to be

played by the private, not-for-profit, and governmental sectors, in a pluralistic society such as ours.

3. Create a new "generalist" practitioner who can perform a variety of functions, and suggest an appropriate educational curriculum for the preparation of such individuals.

4. Suggest several locations, both in statewide and local structures, where such an individual may be employed.

Thus, the HSW is perceived to be a professional human services generalist, who can be employed in several locations, and who will work with existing human service agencies which may be sponsored by governmental bodies, voluntary groups, or for-profit corporations.

The debate over generalist versus specialist practice is an old one in the human services (Austin, 1981, pp. 23–26). The HSW is viewed in this proposal as a generalist because of the wide breadth of knowledge and skills which will be required to perform the five main functions to be discussed below, and because of the wide variety of clients and presenting problems he/she will encounter. Specifically, the HSW will perform the following five functions, which will each be discussed below, in turn:

- Assessment
- Referral
- Client Advocacy
- Coordination
- Evaluation

ASSESSMENT

As Austin has pointed out, all human service programs have an intake component which can include, in addition to determination of eligibility, an assessment (however initial) of the needs of the client (Austin, 1981). Prior to seeing clients for assessment, the HSW should thoroughly familiarize himself/herself with the community resources available (Day, 1989)—to which the client may be referred for specialized service (more detailed discussion of the referral function will be discussed below).

After becoming well-versed in community resources, the HSW should also consider local demographics. Is this community composed of a multiracial, multiethnic, multireligious, multiage population? If so, are certain groups more likely to come to the agency for service than others? If they are, then can the HSW improve communication during the assessment process by becoming familiar with the community's respective predominant foreign languages, customs, etc., in advance? Such efforts will likely reduce the "distance" between client and provider and enhance the assessment process (Green, 1982).

After the above preparations have been made, the HSW should view the client from a holistic standpoint, taking into account physical, psychological, economic, and social needs (Huttman, 1981, p. 21). And the historical attempts to *separate* the intrapsychic and social variables impacting on a client's problems, currently under intense criticism, should be avoided when assessing the presenting (and subsequent) problems (Vigilante and Mailick, 1988).

The assessment process is normally begun with the accumulation of a variety of data by the HSW. In view of the expansive role we propose for the HSW, with five main functions, we recommend the following material be collected:

- Vital statistics: age, gender, race
- Demographic data: marital status, address, occupation, educational level
- Information on the nuclear family members (and extended family, if apropos): names, addresses, occupations, ages, educational levels
- Medical history of the client: hereditary disease, surgeries, illnesses, hospitalizations, physician's name and address
- Financial status of the client: income, pensions, financial aid, etc.
- Past assistance from human service agencies: where, when, why?
- Presenting problem: as perceived by the client

If the client presents more than one problem, the HSW should work with the client to *prioritize* the multiple problems, in the event that they cannot be treated simultaneously, or in case there are limited resources preventing solving all of them expeditiously (Huttman, 1981, p. 37).

It will also be necessary for the HSW to determine the client's *level of functioning*, (Carter and Newman, 1976; Newman and Rinkus, 1978), in order to make an appropriate assessment—and later, referral. McKillip describes one example of a "level of functioning scale" which distinguishes between "dysfunctional" and "functional" clients. Dysfunction may be described as occurring at four levels: (1) the client is dysfunctional in all areas and is almost totally dependent upon others to provide a supportive, protective environment; (2) the client's symptoms are so severe as to render him/her incapable of functioning independently; (3) the client's symptoms are so severe as to require almost constant supervision; (4) and the client's symptoms require consistent intervention. The functional client may be classified at five different levels, as follows: (1) the client has a low stress tolerance, making regular therapeutic intervention advisable; (2) the client's symptoms and their severity are probably sufficient to be both noticeable and somewhat disconcerting to the individual and/or those around him/her in daily contact; (3) the client's symptoms occur sufficiently frequently to maintain reliance on regular therapeutic intervention; (4) the client is functioning well in all areas with little evidence of distress; and (5) the client is functioning well in all areas with no treatment/referral recommended (McKillip, 1987, p. 37).

In sum, the assessment function of the HSW is a vital one, for the remaining four functions to be discussed all reflect the validity of the assessment process. That validity may be enhanced if there is minimal "distance" between the HSW and the client in their communication, the HSW takes a holistic, systems view of the client and his/her problem, the HSW is well versed in community resources and can make an appropriate agency referral—after taking into account the client's social, medical, financial, and psychological history; current level of functioning; and prioritization of presenting problems. And because we agree with Huttman that needs change over time, and new needs arise, on return visits to the HSW for reassessment, care should be taken to update the client's file and review the level of functioning, prioritization of needs, and other relevant aspects of the process (Huttman, 1981, p. 37).

REFERRAL

Once the HSW has assessed the intake data and reached agreement on the identification of the problem, with the client, referral for treatment will be made. If more than one problem has been diagnosed, then the problem will be prioritized and handled as expeditiously as possible, depending upon logistics, availability of resources, and related issues. In this capacity, the HSW is serving as a "gatekeeper" to services (Meddin, 1982).

As mentioned above, in order to make appropriate referrals, the HSW must be thoroughly familiar with community resources. Material for use in referral may come from a variety of sources—governmental, voluntary, for-profit. Various governmental agencies associated with health and social service functions (including public health and welfare agencies) publish and distribute literature on their services. Voluntary organizations do the same thing—an example of which is a directory of health and medical resources published by the Palm Beach County Medical Association (Palm Beach County Medical Association, 1988). Sometimes the specific needs of a community generate directories of services. One of the authors of this volume coedited such a directory for a new "model city" built on midwestern farmland. The directory was needed as the new town was being populated by strangers who had no idea where available health services were located. The effort was jointly sponsored by a group of volunteers who were trying to establish a new hospital in the area, and the entrepreneurial developer of the new town (Bateson and Richie, 1973). And in South Florida, which has a significant population of elderly needing long-term care, a commercial publisher has distributed a directory on nursing home care (Alperin, 1979).

A comprehensive library of agencies/services for referral could include the following, depending on community resources (Riley, 1981, p. 94; DiNitto and Dye, 1987, p. 3):

- Financial assistance
- Housing
- Food
- Jobs
- Adoption
- Services for unmarried parents
- Foster placement services
- Travelers aid
- Homemaker services
- Debt/credit counseling
- Friendly visiting
- Protective services
- Psychological testing
- Mental health clinics
- Alcoholism treatment
- Day care centers
- Big brother/big sister programs
- Institutional services
- Drug abuse treatment
- Meals on wheels
- Legal aid services

- Summer camp programs
- Foster placement of adults

The treatment modalities/techniques offered by such agencies may also be of considerable variety, and should be known to the HSW at the time of referral. These may include (Riley, 1981, pp. 92–93):

- Family group treatment
- Group therapy
- Cotherapy in groups or family treatment
- Planned short-term treatment
- Behavior modification techniques
- Transactional analysis
- Sex therapy
- Parent effectiveness training
- Gestalt therapy
- Marriage enrichment groups
- Written client contracts
- Use of videotape playbacks
- Structured communication training
- Multifamily group treatment
- Crisis intervention
- Group intake
- Marathon groups
- Encounter and/or sensitivity groups
- Multiple impact therapy
- Family life education/family enrichment

It is important to reiterate that the client is likely to have more than one problem. One study divided problems into seven main types: marital; children; individual adjustment; environmental; family; home management; and major social/behavioral (such as alcoholism, drug abuse, mental illness). Using this typology, the researchers found an average of four problems per family in their sample (Beck and Jones, 1973).

The compendium of information collected by the HSW on community agencies/services is referred to by McKillip as a "resource inventory"— "the services available to one or more target groups, usually in a specific geographic area" (McKillip, 1987, p. 32).

Another tool for use by the HSW is the typology of human services developed by the United Way of America—the United Way of America Services Identification System II (Sumariwalla, 1976). The system identifies, classifies and defines individual, organized human endeavors in relation to major goals of society. Eight general goals form the core of the system:

- Optimal income security and economic opportunity
- Optimal health
- Optimal provision of basic material needs
- Optimal opportunity for the acquisition of knowledge and skills
- Optimal environmental quality
- Optimal individual and collective safety
- Optimal social functioning
- Optimal assurance of the support and effectiveness of services through organized actions

In addition to using this typology in referring clients, the HSW may also use it as a standard against which to measure community resources. Where significant deficiencies occur in a given community, the HSW may try to agitate for the development of needed services. This issue will be further discussed in the next section, on client advocacy.

Along with having a comprehensive resource inventory at his/her disposal, the HSW must also have functional communication networks (especially with heavily-used agencies) in order to cut through some of the bureaucratic red tape which can delay referral/treatment. As Toffler has recently pointed out, nonhierarchical communications networks are proliferating, in this time of rapid dissemination of information and rapid change—on both the personal and societal levels (Toffler, 1990).

After agreement has been reached between the HSW and client on the problem/problems and agency/agencies to which referral will be made, an informed consent should be obtained from the client, indicating he/she has no objection to the referral(s), and agrees to the sharing of information with the agencies to which referral is being made. The informed consent should specify why the referral is being made, to whom, and the type of information to be shared. This action is recommended not only to reduce future liability in the courts, but also to authorize the HSW to perform the other functions to be discussed: advocacy, coordination, and evaluation (Pozgar, 1990, pp. 116–130; Rosoff, 1980).

CLIENT ADVOCACY

Under the First Amendment of the U.S. Constitution, citizens have the right to lobby their legislators for causes/position they advocate. In the delivery of human services, unfortunately, clients are often especially vulnerable and unable to effectively pursue their own best interests without professional assistance. The HSW is in an excellent position to assist in this process (Sunley, 1983).

The discussion (above) of client dissatisfaction with the human service system, listed the major complaints clients have expressed during research into this issue. Peirce finds it especially distressful that clients often are blamed for failing to function, when the system itself is inadequate (Peirce, 1974). Three ways in which the HSW can engage in client advocacy are as follows:

• Reduce barriers for clients referred to particularly bureaucratic and/or large agencies, via telephone or written correspondence with staff at the respective agencies

• Assist the client who does not meet all eligibility requirements (*prior* to referral, if the problem is known and manageable)

• Identify deficiencies in the local human services system, and in concert with other professionals and clients, advocate for their provision

Pearlman and Edwards view the advocacy model as a synthesis of ego psychology and systems theory—within an ecological framework. Thus, it is a professional service that provides the client and practitioner with an alternative approach to understanding and dealing with problems associated with adverse or dysfunctional systems or institutional practices. In the practice of client advocacy, clients should be helped to develop their own means to affect change in institutional practices impacting negatively on them (Pearlman and Edwards, 1982). And Feld has pointed out that advocacy can be viewed as a form of healing, if it connects needful clients with appropriate services (Feld, 1991).

With some clients, attempts to assist and encourage them in pressing for their rights in the human service system involve considerable effort on the part of the HSW. This will often be due to a feeling of "powerlessness"—which Pinderhughes attributes to a variety of factors with which many clients have to deal: crime; violence; incest; alcoholism; drug addiction; unemployment; inflation; and reductions-in-service. The result of such a history can be an overwhelming sense of being unable to control one's destiny. Empowerment of the client thus involves assisting the client to develop the capacity to influence the forces affecting his/her life space—for personal benefit (Pinderhughes, 1983).

While the client advocacy role discussed here, for the HSW, is described on an individual or family level, human services professionals working in other settings, with groups or communities, can establish "client advocacy groups" and apply the same principles (Pearlman and Edwards, 1982).

COORDINATION

As indicated above, the large number of human service agencies, and the specialized services offered by many of them, can lead to confusion, gaps in services, and even unnecessary duplication of services. Between 1960–1980, the number of human services professionals grew by 242 percent, while during that same period, specialization also increased (Reisch and Wenocur, 1984). This fragmentation of services is often accompanied by a lack of planning and problem-solving, and tends to be agency-oriented, rather than client-oriented. Thus, a "network" must be created that produces "intervention aimed at promoting a collaborative, problem-solving approach to human service problems" (Novick, 1990). The HSW is ideally suited to play such a role, in order that the interacting parts of the human services system are *truly* coordinated, as per the definition of "system" being used here.

In the model presented here, the HSW works within the existant local human services system, and with a variety of agencies having varying sponsorship/goals—as opposed to a model based on large, monolithic bureaucracies. In this regard, Toffler has recently proposed that the future holds a proliferation of small organizations which will interact on an ad-hoc basis to create "temporary mosaics," in order to address specific problems/goals. He sees such a model as more adaptive, and ultimately more productive, than one based on a limited number of rigid monoliths (Toffler, 1990).

Thus, an additional function of the HSW will be to coordinate treatment—after the client has been assessed, referred, and represented through advocacy action. In the course of so doing, the HSW will help improve the interaction among community agencies, as well as that between the client and the various agencies to which he/she has been referred (Abels and Murphy, 1981). Aiding the HSW in these tasks will be the new management information systems (MIS) technology—which is computer-based, and increasingly available at competitive costs to agencies. As indicated earlier, because of possible litigation over the types of material collected, stored, and shared, professional procedures regarding confidentiality and informed consent will have to be respected (Gruber et al., 1984).

The coordination function of the HSW is not unrelated to that of a "case manager"—one who has responsibility for monitoring the process and outcome of the delivery of human services in an era of increased specialization (Stern and Gibelman, 1990). Federal legislation in 1981 enabled states to pay for case management for Medicaid recipients under waiver of the usual rules—illustrating the importance of the function (Barker, 1987). Traditionally, case management has been viewed as composed of seven components (Austin, 1981):

- Evaluating the need or request
- Determining client eligibility
- Planning for the provision and/or arrangement of services
- Arranging for the delivery of services
- Providing services
- Overseeing services
- Recording progress toward service goals

In the HSW model presented here, components 1–3 (above) fall under Assessment, 4 and 5 under Referral and Client Advocacy, 6 under Coordination, and 7 under Evaluation (to be discussed below).

The HSW, in performing the Coordination function, improves the human services system in his/her community by taking the *inputs* obtained at Assessment and processing them as *throughputs* (via Referral, Advocacy and Coordination) until *outputs* are obtained, via *feedback*—and subjected to Evaluation. Figure 3 illustrates the process (Abels and Murphy, 1981, p. 49).

FIGURE 3 THE SYSTEMS VIEW OF THE HUMAN SERVICES WORKER'S FUNCTIONS

Inputs	Throughputs/Process	Outputs
(Assessment)	(Referral, Advocacy, Coordination)	(Feedback of Results)

Evaluation

The coordination of the client's treatment, through appropriate specialized human service agencies, is illustrated by Figure 4 (Abels and Murphy, 1981, p. 53).

FIGURE 4 COORDINATION OF THE CLIENT'S TREATMENT BY THE HSW

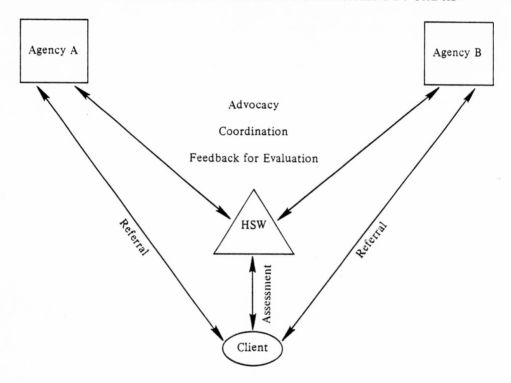

EVALUATION

Evaluation of *medical care* services has existed in some form from the earliest of times. Such evaluations were closely tied to sanctions in ancient times. In Egypt around 3000 BC, for instance, if a patient were to unnecessarily lose an eye, the physician was subject to the loss of a hand (Shortell and Richardson, 1978, pp. 1–2). However, there was little in the way of *formal* evaluation of health and social services prior to the eighteenth century. With the development of a period of revolution and enlightenment in the eighteenth century, came the first major thrust of experimentation and evaluation of public service programs, and these activities have accelerated in recent times (Suchman, 1967, pp. 13–18).

Evaluation in the human services can be variously defined, but most definitions include the notion that it is "an effort to determine what changes have occurred as the result of a planned service program—by comparing *actual* results with *desired* results (goals and objectives), and by identifying the degree to which the program is responsible for the difference" (Abels and Murphy, 1981, p. 138). Important notions contained in this definition include the collection of data, the comparison of these data with a standard or desired result, and a judgment about the outcome (Smith, 1990).

Evaluation is a *process,* taking place in stages, over time. The steps involved, and their relationship to the HSW in his/her multifunctioning role, are as follows (Rubinson and Neutens, 1987, pp. 153–157):

• Determining who is the client: the client may be an individual, a couple, or a whole family. During the assessment phase, the HSW will identify the client.

• Determining what will be the purpose of the evaluation: this will be related directly to the goals/objectives which will be mutually determined by the HSW and client(s) during the ASSESSMENT/INTAKE process. As mentioned earlier, there may be multiple problems which will require prioritization. Likewise, multiple goals may need to be prioritized, if it is unrealistic to achieve them simultaneously.

• Determining what kind of methodology will be used: the methodology will be dependent upon a number of variables, including the nature of the problem, the type of data to be collected, personal characteristics of the client(s), the nature of the agencies to which referral is being made, etc.

• Determining clearly the responsibilities of all the players in the process: what role will be played in the evaluation process by the client(s), the HSW, and staff at the agencies to which referral is made?

• Determining how the evaluation will be conducted: what data will be supplied by the client, HSW, and community agencies? How will the data be transmitted, collected, analyzed?

• Determining who will use the results of the evaluation: what safeguards will be taken to protect clients' rights to confidentiality/privacy? What use will be made of the data? How will the feedback mechanism operate?

As the role of the HSW has been described above, the following data sets will be available for use in the evaluation process (Green et al., 1980, pp. 132–141):

- Demographic and personal history data
- Medical history
- Behavioral data
- Client perceptions of the problem(s)
- Client perceptions of the goal(s)
- Information on past treatment from the human services system

Obviously, some of the above data are more easily quantifiable than others. In medicine, quantitative parameters have been established for a variety of conditions—although there is still, admittedly, a qualitative element to holistic health which is receiving greater emphasis by researchers as time passes (Flagle, 1972). Thus, it is generally easier to measure physical health than mental health (Williams, 1972). When it comes to measuring behavioral objectives, however, one is working largely with qualitative data, which are more difficult to test for validity. Traditionally, in the human services, single-case interventions have been used for evaluation. In these instances, qualitative case studies are the primary methodology for determining the efficacy of treatment. Single-case interventions can focus on couples or families—as well as individuals (Tripodi, 1983, pp. 100–120).

Since therapy is a *process,* there are varying points during the client-HSW interaction at which evaluation can take place (Abels and Murphy, 1981, p. 139):

- Intake evaluation: assessment of the intake data and determination of the problem for which referral will be made is part of the evaluation process.

- On-going evaluation: assessment of the client-HSW interaction at intake, during the referral process to community agencies, and in regard to the HSW's attempts at client advocacy and coordination, are all examples of evaluation which takes place in an on-going manner.

- Outcome evaluation: do the results of the client's treatment coincide with stated goals/objectives? Goals, which may be short-term or long-term (Austin, 1981, pp. 104–105) are *general* statements of desired outcomes, while objectives are much more *specific* statements—usually consistent with the broader goals. The specification of measureable goals/objectives, in advance, and their later evaluation, has long been advocated by Peter Drucker in his development of the "management by objectives" process. Here, each person being evaluated creates a set of objectives, in concert with his/her supervisor, which can be later measured, after a specified time period. All such objectives should be consistent with the agency's broader goals. A similar process can be used between the client and the HSW, as one model for goal-setting (Drucker, 1954; Deegan and O'Donovan, 1982; Rakich et al., 1985, pp. 393–394; Rubinson and Neutens, 1987, pp. 160–162).

Coincident with determination of whether agreed-upon goals have been achieved, in the planned manner and expected time frame, will be the need to determine if the HSW should consider the case "closed" (Austin, 1981, p. 108). A variety of outcomes are possible, including:

• The client's problem(s) seems to be sufficiently under control, so that no further treatment is currently needed. In this case, during the termination interview, the HSW should be certain that the client is satisfied, aware of symptoms which may reappear—signaling recidivism, and clear on procedures for reestablishing contact with the HSW. Even if the problem does not reappear, a follow-up study may be in order at a later date (Beck and Jones, 1974).

• Some of the client's multiple problems may have been satisfactorily resolved, while others continue under treatment.

• New problems may have emerged which require assessment/treatment.

• The client prematurely discontinues treatment, and efforts to reengage him/her are unsuccessful.

• Program impact evaluation: is the introduction of the HSW into the local human services system an effective way to improve services to the target population? This particular evaluation, while including input from the HSW, would most likely be conducted by another party, for the sake of objectivity (Windsor et al., 1984). Feedback from the agencies to which the HSW refers clients is another data source on the efficacy of the HSW model. This feedback may be obtained using data collection techniques common in the social sciences, such as personal and/or telephone interviews, mail questionnaires/surveys (Rubinson and Neutens, 1987, pp. 152–190).

Among the advantages of evaluation in the human services are the following:

• The fact that program evaluation promotes *consumerism*, in that clients of programs are asked directly about the usefulness of programs (Smith, 1990, p. 24).

• The fact that the multifaceted nature of human problems is likely to be uncovered and addressed during the evaluation process. One study that evaluated 28 family service agencies found them burdened with multiproblem client-families, who often felt helpless and beseiged by the multiplicity of pressures/problems impacting them (Minahan, 1987, pp. 592–593).

• The fact that the process leaves room for evaluation by *both* client and provider, and the points at which those respective evaluations converge/diverge are of considerable interest. Beck and Jones, for instance, examined this issue in a nationwide survey which took into account both the counselor's rating of treatment outcomes *and* the client's. Global ratings were made along four points: much better; somewhat better; no change (or mixed); worse. The methodology used in the study has applications in other settings as well (Beck and Jones, 1973).

• The fact that program evaluation allows for both the improvement of human services *and* innovations (Windsor et al., 1984, p. 18). The implementation of the HSW in a given community setting, and the later evaluation of this "new" professional role, would be an example of innovation in the human services.

Among the problems to be addressed in human services evaluation are the following:

• The fact that outcome measurement in the human services is still difficult because of the qualitative and multidimensional nature of many of the problems to be addressed. In addition, task-oriented evaluations are generally easier to conduct than behavior-modification evaluations. Complicating this is the problem of obtaining a "control group" which has the same, but untreated, problems. In this case, ethical issues arise when one withholds treatment from the control group. One solution to this problem may be to use groups on "waiting lists" as the control group—providing their reason for being on the waiting list is simply because of a lack of treatment resources at that time (Riley, 1981, pp. 98–99; Kahn, 1984, p. 72).

• The fact that the setting of objectives to be realized can be hampered by vagueness, or undue coercion by one or more participants in the process (Gruber, 1984, pp. 127–128).

• The fact that the HSW may present a "threat" to community agencies to which referral is being made, if they believe the HSW's evaluation function is an attempt to make them look "bad" (Green and Lewis, 1986, p. 8). Thus, it will be necessary to allay the fears of such agencies, in advance, by taking the time to gain their confidence and cooperation. Such agencies can be involved in the development of evaluation documents, completion and forwarding of said documents to the HSW, and interpretation of the results.

Now that the role and primary functions of the HSW have been described, we shall turn to a discussion of locations in the human services system where such an individual may be employed.

LOCATION OF THE
HUMAN SERVICES WORKER IN THE SYSTEM

When the HSW model was introduced (above) we pointed out that our proposal attempted to *modify* rather than dramatically change, the current human services system. The rationale for modification, rather than a system overhaul, was based on pragmatic political, economic, and social factors and trends. So too, when proposing where to locate the HSW in the system, we are using as our "best" example one which we believe can be implemented with minimal disruption of the current systems, and with manageable additional expense—through the use of current resources and organizational structures.

As Freeman has pointed out, innovations (and we consider the HSW, as here described, to be an innovation) are adopted and persist only when they are consistent with the structural arrangements in a society (Freeman, 1972). The structural readiness which he describes as necessary for the incorporation to be made already exists, with some variation, in the respective states. In the State of Florida, the Department of Health and Rehabilitative Services (HRS) is the agency which could easily incorporate the HSW, to carry out the five functions described above, in order to bring a combination of governmental, voluntary and for-profit services to clients—not only because the agency has traditionally encountered many of the neediest, multiproblem clients, but also because a statewide organizational structure already exists. While some of the human services problems addressed in Florida are directly related to its demographic, geographic and economic idiosyncrasies, the Florida Chapter of the National Association of Social Workers, after comparing the respective states on their approach to addressing such problems, views Florida as a bellwether state, where innovations have encouraged other states to be more proactive and innovative (Florida Chapter of the National Association of Social Workers, January 1991).

While this proposal uses a Florida-state agency as an example, it should be pointed out that each state provides, in some fashion, for the provision of human services. The Council of State Governments has developed a four-part typology of the comprehensive human resources departments found in the various American states. They are as follows (Council of State Governments, 1974; Page, 1988):

• State Categorical Agency: where one major function or a limited array of closely-related functions is performed.

• Confederated Agency: where each programmatic entity has a separate unit for its own planning, evaluation, budgeting, administrative support, field structure for service delivery, and external relations with interest groups and legislative bodies.

• Consolidated Agency: where most or all programming functions and administrative authorities are transferred to a new, more unified organization.

• Integrated State Human Service Agency: where a general systems approach is used to link organizational units, programs, communication channels in an interdependent fashion.

We believe that appropriate modifications can be made in any of these models to incorporate the HSW proposal made herein.

In 1969, the Florida HRS was created along with twenty other state agencies by the Government Reorganization Act. It was not until 1975, however, that HRS emerged in much the same form that it is today. As established by Section 20.19 of the Florida Statutes, two of the key concepts behind its organizational structure are the *integration of services* and *decentralized authority* (Committee on Health and Rehabilitative Services, December 6, 1990; Florida Statute 20.19, 1989). The primary goals of HRS are as follows (Department of Health and Rehabilitative Services, January, 1984):

• Create opportunities for client economic independence and self-sufficiency.

• Make available an appropriate range of services to all HRS clients.

• Emphasize cost-effective prevention services in all HRS programs.

• Ensure the quality of care and treatment in HRS institutions.

• Ensure the quality of care and treatment in HRS-operated and purchased community programs.

• Improve and expand services to elderly and disabled adults.

• Improve and expand services to children, youth, and families at risk.

• Improve delivery of essential health services.

- Improve public understanding of, and involvement in, HRS programs and services.
- Improve the efficiency, effectiveness and productivity of administration and operations.
- Improve the results of the department's affirmative action plan.
- Enhance employee morale and job satisfaction.
- Establish cooperative working relationships with other agencies and organizations, public and private, in order to improve services.

As can be seen from a close examination of the above-stated goals, many are consistent with the role which has been already described for the HSW.

As presently constituted, HRS offers programs in eight main categories (Department of Health and Rehabilitative Services, July 1988):

- Aging and Adult Services (for those age 60 and over, and for disabled adults of any age).
- Alcohol, Drug Abuse, and Mental Health Treatment.
- Children's Medical Services.
- Children, Youth, and Families (help for families with problems affecting their children).
- Developmental Services (for people who have developmental disabilities).
- Economic Services (food stamps and financial help for eligible persons).
- Health Services (public health services provided largely through county public health units, as well as regulation of health facilities).
- Medicaid (payment for medical care and treatment).

HRS carries out its mandate under the direction of a secretary who has an assistant secretary directing each of the eight programs listed above (Department of Health and Rehabilitative Services, July 1990a). The State is divided into eleven districts, and the organization of services varies somewhat by district—depending upon whether the district is urban/rural, densely/sparsely populated, geographically small/large (Department of Health and Rehabilitative Services, July 1990b). The Department's budget in Fiscal Year 1990–1991 was $7.5 billion—making it the second largest state agency, after the Department of Education (Associated Press, 1990).

By coincidence, the proposal being made herein—that HSWs be hired to work in each HRS district, performing the five functions described earlier—is being made at a time when HRS is under considerable scrutiny to improve its operations. Included among other recent criticisms are that: HRS suffers from a top-heavy bureaucracy (Cooper, January 18, 1991); that *local* communities should take greater charge of the operation of human services provided by HRS (Bramstedt, January 18, 1991); and that HRS uses an outdated data system, which must be modernized in order to improve communication and efficiency (Sun-Sentinel Editorial, January 20, 1991). In fact, a specific proposal, utilizing the *voluntary,* not-for-profit sector has recently been made to address some of the problems of HRS, a *governmental* agency. In this proposal, a "Health and Human Services Planning Association" would be created in Palm Beach County, Florida, which would operate in a nonprofit manner, and whose functions would include assessing community needs, and collecting data for use by local agencies—functions which can be filled, at least in part, by the HSW model proposed herein (Cooper, June 8, 1990). Thus, the HSW model can also be incorporated into nonprofit agencies, although for the reasons listed above, we believe its quickest incorporation would likely occur in state agencies of the HRS-type. While there is nothing preventing the for-profit sector from engaging the HSW, the closest model discussed in this volume, from that sector, would probably be the Employee Assistance Program Worker in corporations. An HSW could be hired by large corporations with EAPs to perform the respective functions. It is also possible for an HSW in private practice to perform this role for governmental, voluntary, and proprietary agencies/organizations. And in his review of the cooperative arrangements hospitals of all types (governmental, nonprofit, and proprietary) have enjoyed in recent years in this country—sharing services of various kinds—Williamson inspires us to suggest that such cooperative ventures (consortia, mergers, etc.) could also employ HSWs to perform the functions described above (Williamson, 1986).

Our emphasis here on the incorporation of the HSW into statewide human services networks, such as Florida's HRS, is based on our perception of its being a cost-effective option, which can be incorporated into an existing structure relatively rapidly. This does not preclude those with an interest in the model from pursuing its incorporation in other settings/locations. One such alternative is to locate the HSW in public-school settings. A recent report cites initial Congressional interest in a "one-stop shopping" approach to human services—especially for poor children and their families—by providing professional assistance in health care, job training, early-childhood, adult education, and welfare services in a convenient location, such as the public schools. Demonstration projects have found such an approach helpful in assisting hard-to-reach, hard-to-teach populations, such as drug-abusing mothers, and youths from economically-depressed neighborhoods (Zaldivar, 1991). An HSW could be employed in such a setting to perform the functions described above.

Now that the HSW's role and functions have been described, as well as suggestions offered for location of the HSW in the human services system, there remains the question of how best to prepare HSWs for this role. It is to this question that we now turn.

PROPOSALS FOR THE EDUCATION/TRAINING OF THE HSW

Now that the role, functions and possible locations of employment for the HSW have been examined, it is necessary to discuss how best to prepare individuals who wish to work in this capacity. The three traditional routes—degree programs, continuing education, and certificates—will be discussed.

Degree Programs

The Bachelor of Social Work (BSW) professional foundation curriculum, endorsed by the Council on Social Work Education (CSWE), encompasses five major areas (Council on Social Work Education, 1981; Griffin and Eure, 1985): Human Behavior and Social Environment; Social Welfare Policy and Services; Social Work Practice; Research; and Field Practicum. These areas would appear to provide an appropriate foundation for the five functions to be performed by the HSW. Because of the wide-ranging scope of clients and problems which the HSW will likely encounter, and the numerous functions to be performed, we would also endorse the *generalist* practice model in the preparation of future HSWs (Teigsler, 1983). Even when the authors of this volume examined social workers in three "unique" settings—hospices, continuing/life care facilities, and community-based AIDS services agencies—they discovered the generalist core to be the best preparation, with the addition of selected elective courses relevant to each respective setting. In the case of hospice social work, elective courses in psychology/counseling were particularly recommended; in regard to continuing/life care services, elective courses in gerontology/geriatrics were recommended; and in the case of AIDS services agencies, electives in public health, epidemiology, stress management and communication were considered particularly relevant (Alperin, 1985; Alperin and Richie, 1988; Alperin and Richie, 1989; Alperin and Richie, 1991).

Green has indicated that sometimes the relevant electives will be courses that reduce the "distance" between clients and providers—such as foreign languages and anthropology. In such cases, the elective courses are more relevant to the target population than the agency's services/structure itself (Green, 1982). And Pearlman and Edwards, in their analysis of the client advocacy function, clearly show the overlap between CSWE-recommended foundation courses and relevant electives by stating that the human services practitioner who practices client advocacy needs knowledge of: human growth and development; psychosocial theories; family process; group process; planning; and evaluation (Pearlman and Edwards, 1982).

Table 2 illustrates how preparation for the five main functions of the HSW may be achieved by the CSWE's foundation curriculum—plus relevant electives.

Optimistic projections for the growth of the social work profession in the 1990s, including the U.S. Labor Department's report that employment of social workers is expected to increase faster on average than for all occupations through the year 2000, in response to the needs of a growing and aging population (Kleiman, 1990), suggest that currently-established BSW programs are likely to be the best locus for finding, and preparing, future HSWs. If the role described in this volume is accepted by professional educators and employers, students in BSW programs may be recruited to prepare for the role by augmenting their foundation courses with relevant electives—pertinent to the particular social/racial/ethnic/religious communities in which they plan to seek employment. Thus, without the necessity for creating a totally *new* degree (with its concomitant political and cost disincentives) current BSW-accredited programs should be able to easily prepare the future HSW, through judicious selection of elective courses.

Of course, other degrees (both undergraduate and graduate) currently in existence may also be amenable to incorporation of the curriculum described above, although perhaps not so readily as in the case of accredited BSW programs (Brawley, 1981). Curriculum issues are a com-

Table 2. Educational Preparation for Fulfilling the Human Services Worker's Functions.

Functions	CSWE Foundation Areas	Relevant Electives
Assessment	Human Behavior and Social Environment Social Work Practice Research Field Practicum	Foreign Languages Anthropology Psychology Counseling Economics
Referral	Social Work Policy and Services Social Work Practice Research	Anthropology Psychology Counseling
Client Advocacy	Human Behavior and Social Environment Social Welfare Policy and Services Social Work Practice	Psychology Political Science
Coordination	Social Welfare Policy and Services	Management Systems Theory Sociology
Evaluation	Research Field Practicum	Statistics Strategic Planning

plex field of study in and of themselves, as evidenced, for example, by a recent examination of the question of how best to prepare a human services worker to *administer* such an agency. When curricula from three different degree programs (Master of Business Administration—MBA, Master of Public Administration—MPA, and Master of Social Work—MSW) were examined, the answer proved to be far from simple. The degrees studied provided a continuum for management in the human services, whereby the MBA contributes skill and knowledge from the realm of finance; the MPA contributes heavily to functioning in public-sector planning organizations of the type often seen in public social welfare agencies; and the MSW contributes skills and knowledge that are appropriate to human services delivery organizations in which the client interacts with the institution (Cupaiuolo and Miringoff, 1988). We believe there is sufficient room to experiment with curricula designed to provide the competencies needed by HSWs to fulfill the five functions described above in the performance of their role, and encourage such experimentation.

Continuing Education

"Continuing education" refers to formal education obtained after completing a degree. Such education is usually intended to improve or maintain the professional's competence. Some, but not all, states require a specified number of hours of recognized continuing education units (CEUs) per specified time period, as a condition of continued licensure (Goldstein, 1989, p. 58; U.S. House of Representatives, February 1976, p. 37).

The need for continuing education for professionals has become increasingly acute in recent years, as rapid developments in technology, and new knowledge, have exploded on the American scene. One's professional skills can become at least "semi-obsolete" in a relatively short time (Toffler, 1970; Houle, 1980).

Concern has been expressed for some time over the large number of human services workers without appropriate degrees. A study of HRS employees in the State of Florida indicated that only 3 percent had degrees in social work (Florida Chapter National Association of Social Workers, January 1991). While this is not necessarily the case in all human services settings, there are believed to be many degreed human services workers nationwide without appropriate formal training in the human services. Continuing education is a formal mechanism by which they (and holders of social work degrees, also) may accumulate the necessary competencies to perform the functions of an HSW. For the social work degree holder, continuing education in relevant electives, such as those listed in Table 2, may be sufficient preparation for the role of the HSW. For human services employees without social work degrees, the accumulation of college credits in some, or all, of the five CSWE-recommended foundation areas—plus relevant electives, may be necessary.

Certificate Programs

It is not uncommon for professional schools to establish specialized curricula and offer *certificates* in the respective areas. These programs are usually easier to authorize and less expensive to operate than new degree programs (Stoesz, 1989). In keeping with the notion that a generic professional base is appropriate for the HSW, a certificate approach is another educational-preparation possibility. In this instance, a school of social work would award a certificate to holders of bachelor's degrees, who had completed all relevant courses (required and elective). Some prospective students may find the opportunity to earn a certificate to be a greater incentive to return to school than simply the accumulation of CEUs through a variety of separate continuing education courses.

The role, functions, employment locations and educational preparation of the HSW have now been discussed. The human services system in which such a professional would work has often been a reactive one, relying heavily on crisis intervention. If we are to take a more proactive stance in regard to the human services, it will be necessary to place greater emphasis on long-range planning (Health and Rehabilitative Services, 1989). With this in mind, we turn in Part IV to a discussion of several human services areas which we believe will require special attention over the coming decade, as we approach the next millenium.

REFERENCES

Abels, Paul and Michael Murphy. *Administration in the Human Services: A Normative Systems Approach.* Englewood Cliffs, NJ: Prentice-Hall, 1981.

Alperin, Diane E. "Hospice Social Work: Support for Generalist Training," *Social Work in Health Care,* Vol. 10, No. 3, Spring 1985, pp. 119–122.

Alperin, Diane E. and Nicholas D. Richie. "Social Services in Continuing/Life Care Communities: Implications for Social Work Education," *Arete,* Vol. 13, No. 1, Summer 1988, pp. 29–34.

Alperin, Diane E. and Nicholas D. Richie. "Community-Based AIDS Service Organizations: Challenges and Educational Preparation," *Health and Social Work,* Vol. 14, No. 3, 1989, pp. 165–173.

Alperin, Diane E. and Nicholas D. Richie. "Comprehensive Care in Community-Based AIDS Services Agencies." *AIDS Patient Care,* Vol. 5, No. 5, October 1991.

Alperin, Sondra P. (ed.). *A Guide Book to Florida Nursing Homes.* Miami: U.S. Directory Service, 1979.

Associated Press. "Chiles Inspects HRS, Will Seek 'Miracle Worker'." Ft. Lauderdale, FL: *Sun-Sentinel,* November 30, 1990, p. 23A.

Austin, Michael. *Supervisory Management for the Human Services.* Englewood Cliffs, NJ: Prentice-Hall, 1981.

Barker, Robert L. "Case Management," in *The Social Work Dictionary.* Silver Spring, MD: National Association of Social Workers, 1987.

Bateson, Jan and Nicholas Richie (eds.). *A Directory of Health Services for Park Forest South and the South Suburbs.* Park Forest South, IL: New Community Enterprises, 1973.

Beck, Dorothy Fahs and Mary Ann Jones. *Progress on Family Problems — A Nationwide Study of Clients' and Counselors' Views on Family Agency Services.* New York: Family Service Association of America, 1973.

Beck, Dorothy Fahs and Mary Ann Jones. *How to Conduct a Client Follow-Up Study.* New York: Family Service Association of America, 1974.

Berger, P. and R.J. Neuhaus. *To Empower People.* Washington, DC: American Enterprise Institute, 1977.

Blumenstein, Henry. "Survival Issues Challenging Family Agencies," *Social Casework,* Vol. 69, No. 2, February 1988, pp. 107–115.

Boyer, Ruth. *An Approach to the Human Services.* San Francisco: Canfield Press/Harper and Row, 1975.

Brager, George and Stephen Holloway. *Changing Human Service Organizations.* New York: Free Press, 1978.

Bramstedt, Connie. "HRS Official Rips Agency Practices." Ft. Lauderdale, FL: *Sun-Sentinel,* January 18, 1991, p. 7B.

Brawley, Edward A. "Human Service Education Programs: Their Nature and Significance for Social Work," *Journal of Education for Social Work,* Vol. 17, No. 3, Fall 1981, pp. 90–97.

Breslow, Lester. "Consumer-Defined Goals for the Health Care Systems of the 1980s," in *Technology and Health Care Systems in the 1980s,* U.S.D.H.E.W., National Center for Health Services, DHEW Pub. No. HRA-74-3016, Washington, DC: GPO, 1972, pp. 113–123.

Carter, D.E. and F.L. Newman. *A Client-Oriented System of Mental Health Services Delivery and Program Management.* Government Document 017-024-00523-1. Washington, DC: Government Printing Office, 1976.

Clode, Drew, Christopher Parker and Stuart Etherington, (eds.). *Towards the Sensitive Bureaucracy: Consumers, Welfare and the New Pluralism.* Brookfield, VT: Gower, 1987.

Committee on Health and Rehabilitative Services. *Interim Project Report: The Organizational Structure of the Department of HRS.* Tallahassee, FL: The House of Representatives, December 6, 1990.

Consumer Health Services, Inc. *Prologue – America's Most Important Source on Doctors.* Boulder, CO: Cone Communications, 1989.

Consumers Union. "The HMO Approach to Health Care," *Consumer Reports,* May 1982 issue (Educational Reprint).

Consumers Union. *The Medicine Show–Fifth Edition.* Mt. Vernon, NY: Consumers Union, 1983.

Cooper, William. "Agency Proposed to Coordinate County's Social Services Needs." West Palm Beach, FL: *Palm Beach Post,* June 8, 1990, p. 12B.

Cooper, William. "HRS Should be Dismantled, Task Force Told." West Palm Beach, FL: *Palm Beach Post,* January 18, 1991.

Council of State Governments. *Human Services Integration.* Lexington, KY: Council of State Governments, 1974.

Council on Social Work Education. *Curriculum Policy Statement.* New York: Council on Social Work Education, 1981.

Cupaiuolo, Anthony A. and Marc L. Miringoff. "MBA, MPA, MSW: Is There a Degree of Choice for Human Service Management?," in *New Management in*

Human Services, Paul Keys and Leon Ginsberg, (eds.). Silver Spring, MD: National Association of Social Workers, 1988, Chapter 3, pp. 44–57.

Day, Phyllis J. "The New Poor in America: Isolationism in an International Political Economy," *Social Work,* Vol. 34, No. 3, May 1989, pp. 227–233.

Deegan, Arthur and Thomas O'Donovan. *Management by Objectives for Hospitals.* Rockville, MD: Aspen Systems Corporation, 1982.

Department of Health and Rehabilitative Services. *Departmental Goals.* Tallahassee, FL: Department of Health and Rehabilitative Services, January 1984.

Department of Health and Rehabilitative Services. *The Florida Department of Health and Rehabilitative Services.* Tallahassee, FL: Department of Health and Rehabilitative Services, July 1988.

Department of Health and Rehabilitative Services. *Organizational Chart.* Tallahassee, FL: Department of Health and Rehabilitative Services, July 1990a.

Department of Health and Rehabilitative Services. *Overview of HRS Programs and Budget.* Tallahassee, FL: Department of Health and Rehabilitative Services, July 1990b.

DiNitto, D. and T. Dye. *Social Welfare Politics and Public Policy.* Englewood Cliffs, NJ: Prentice-Hall, 1987.

Drucker, Peter. *The Practice of Management.* New York: Harper and Brothers, 1954.

Feld, Karen. "Advocacy Heals," *Headlines: The Brain Injury Magazine.* Spring 1991, pp. 11–16.

Flagle, Charles D. "Evaluation and Control of Technology in Health Services", in *Technology and Health Care Systems in the 1980s,* Morris Collen, (ed.). Washington, DC: U.S.D.H.E.W., January 1972, Chapter 21, pp. 213–224.

Florida Chapter National Association of Social Workers. *Proposal for the Three 'E' Campaign for Human Services—Effort, Efficiency, Effectiveness.* Tallahassee, FL: Florida Chapter National Association of Social Workers, January 1991.

Florida Statute 20.19 (1989). *Department of Health and Rehabilitative Services.*

Freeman, Howard. "Technology and the Human Services Arena," in *Technology and Health Care Systems in the 1980s,* Morris Collen, (ed.). Washington, DC: U.S.D.H.E.W., January 1972, Chapter 7, pp. 75–86.

Friedman, Margaret and Gilbert Churchill, Jr. "Using Consumer Perceptions and a Contingency Approach to Improve Health Care Delivery," *Journal of Consumer Research,* Vol. 13, March 1987, pp. 492–510.

Goldstein, Arnold. *Dictionary of Health Care Administration.* Rockville, MD: Aspen Publishers, Inc. 1989.

Green, James. *Cultural Awareness in the Human Services.* Englewood Cliffs, NJ: Prentice-Hall, 1982.

Green, Lawrence W., Marshall W. Kreuter, Sigrid G. Deeds, Kay B. Partridge. *Health Education Planning: A Diagnostic Approach.* Palo Alto, CA: Mayfield, 1980.

Green, Lawrence W. and Frances Marcus Lewis. *Measurement and Evaluation in Health Education and Health Promotion.* Palo Alto, CA: Mayfield, 1986.

Griffin, J. and G. Eure. "Defining the Professional Foundation in Social Work," *Journal of Social Work Education,* Vol. 21, 1985, pp. 73–91.

Gruber, Murray, Richard Caputo and Thomas Meenaghan. "Information Management," in *Human Services at Risk,* Felice Perlmutter, (ed.)., Lexington, MA: Lexington Books, 1984, Chapter 8, pp. 127–146.

Health and Rehabilitative Services. *Florida State Health Plan: Health Status Goals for Florida for 2000 — Vol. I.* Tallahassee, FL: Department of Health and Rehabilitation Services, 1989.

Hollingshead, August B. and·Frederick C. Redlich. *Social Class and Mental Illness: A Community Study.* New York: John Wiley and Sons, 1958.

Houle, Cyril O. *Continuing Learning in the Professions.* San Francisco: Jossey-Bass, 1980.

Huttman, Elizabeth. *Introduction to Social Policy.* New York: McGraw-Hill, 1981.

Jones, Mary Gardiner and David M. Gardner, (eds.). *Consumerism.* Lexington, MA: Lexington Books, 1976.

Kahn, Ernest. "The Voluntary Sector Can Remain Alive—and Well," in *Human Services at Risk,* Felice Perlmutter, (ed.). Lexington, MA: Lexington Books, 1984, Chapter 4, pp. 57–74.

Klarman, Herbert. *The Economics of Health.* New York: Columbia University Press, 1965.

Kleiman, Carol. "As the '90s Begins, Social Work Grows as a Popular Profession." Delray Beach, FL: *Delray Beach News,* May 28, 1990, p. 8.

Landesman, Herbert. "Is the Concept of Consumer Sovereignty an Adequate Index of Consumer Satisfaction in the Marketplace?," in *Consumerism,* Mary Gardiner Jones and David M. Gardner, (eds.). Lexington, MA: Lexington Books, 1976, Chapter 13, pp. 105–113.

Loudon, David and Albert Della Bitta. *Consumer Behavior.* New York: McGraw-Hill, 1984.

MacStravic, Robin. *Marketing Health Care.* Germantown, MD: Aspen Systems, 1977.

Maloney, Celia. "Consumer Protection on the State Level," in *Consumerism,* Mary Gardiner Jones and David M. Gardner, (eds.). Lexington, MA: Lexington Books, 1976, Chapter 3, pp. 31–34.

Maslow, Abraham H. *Motivation and Personality — Second Edition.* New York: Harper and Row, 1970.

McKillip, Jack. *Need Analysis: Tools for the Human Services and Education.* Beverly Hills: Sage, 1987.

Meddin, Barbara. "Third-Party Vendorship: An Imperative for the 1980s," *Social Casework,* Vol. 63, No. 7, September 1982, PP. 402–407.

Minahan, Anne, (ed.). *Encyclopedia of Social Work — 18th Edition.* Silver Spring, MD: National Association of Social Workers, 1987.

Mitchell, Andrew A., (ed.). *The Effect of Information on Consumer and Market Behavior.* Chicago: American Marketing Association, 1978.

Mott, Vincent. *The American Consumer — Part One.* Florham Park, NJ: Florham Park Press, 1978.

Nader, Ralph, (ed.). *The Consumer and Corporate Authority.* New York: Harcourt Brace Jovanovich, 1973.

Newman, F.L. and A. Rinkus. "Level of Functioning, Clinical Judgment and Mental

Health Service Evaluation," *Evaluation and the Health Professions*, Vol. 1, 1978, pp. 175–194.

Novick, Neil. "Human Service Networking: Collaboration and Prevention," Seminar at Everglades Area Health Education Center, Children's Health Task Force, West Palm Beach, Florida, January 23, 1990.

Page, William J. "Organizational Structure and Service Delivery Arrangements in Human Services," in *Handbook on Human Services Administration*, Jack Rabin and Marcia B. Steinhauer, (eds.)., New York: Marcel Dekker, 1988, Chapter 2, pp. 45–75.

Palm Beach County Medical Society. *Palm Beach County Health Guide '88*. West Palm Beach, Florida: Hayden-Mitchell Publishing, Inc., 1988.

Pearlman, M.H. and M. Edwards. "Enabling in the Eighties: The Client Advocacy Group," *Social Casework*, Vol. 63, No. 9, 532–539, 1982.

Peirce, F.J. "A Functional Perspective of Social Welfare," in *Perspectives on Social Welfare — Second Edition*, Paul Weinberg, (ed.). New York: Macmillan, 1974, pp. 40–47.

Pinderhughes, E.B. "Empowerment for Our Clients and Ourselves," *Social Casework*, Vol. 64, No. 6, 1983, pp. 331–338.

Pozgar, George. *Legal Aspects of Health Care Administration*. Rockville, MD: Aspen, 1990.

Pittle, R. David. "Regulatory Trends at the National Consumer Product Safety Commission," in *Consumerism*, Mary Gardiner Jones and David M. Gardner, (eds.). Lexington, MA: Lexington Books, 1976, Chapter 2, pp. 21–30.

Rakich, Jonathon, Beaufort Longest, and Kurt Darr. *Managing Health Services Organizations*. Philadelphia: W.B. Saunders, 1985.

Reisch, M. and S. Wenocur. "Professionalism and Voluntarism in Social Welfare: Changing Roles and Functions," in *Voluntarism and Social Work Practice*, F. Schwartz, (ed.)., New York: University Press of America, 1984, pp. 1–23.

Rice, Robert. "Change and Continuity in Family Services," *Families in Society: The Journal of Contemporary Human Services*, Vol. 71, No. 1, 1990, pp. 24–31.

Riley, P. "Amalgamated Programs: Social Services Organized Around Population-Problem Groups," in *Handbook of the Social Sciences*, N. Gilbert and H. Specht, (eds.). Englewood-Cliffs, NJ: Prentice-Hall, 1981, pp. 82–101.

Rosoff, Arnold. *Informed Consent: A Guide for Health Care Providers*. Germantown, MD: Aspen Systems Corporation, 1980.

Rubinson, Laurna and James J. Neutens. *Research Techniques for the Health Sciences*. New York: Macmillan, 1987.

Schon, Donald. "Consumerism in Perspective," in *Consumerism*, Mary Gardiner Jones and David M. Gardner, (eds.). Lexington, MA: Lexington Books, 1976, Chapter 1, pp. 1–19.

Shortell, Stephen M. and William C. Richardson. *Health Program Evaluation*. St. Louis: C.V. Mosby, 1978.

Smith, Michael J. *Program Evaluation in the Human Services*. New York: Springer, 1990.

Spencer, William. "Consumer Expectations of Technology," in *Technology and Health*

Care Systems in the 1980s, U.S.D.H.E.W., National Center for Health Services, DHEW Pub. No. HRA-74-3016. Washington, DC: Government Printing Office, 1972.

Stern, Leonard and Margaret Gibelman. "Voluntary Social Welfare Agencies: Trends, Issues, and Prospects," *Families in Society: The Journal of Contemporary Human Services,* Vol 71, No. 1, January 1990, pp. 13–23.

Stoesz, David. "A Theory of Social Welfare," *Social Work,* Vol. 34, No. 2, 1989, pp. 101–107.

Suchman, E. *Evaluative Research: Principles and Practice in Public Service and Social Action Programs.* New York: Russell Sage Foundation, 1967, pp. 13–18.

Sumariwalla, R.D. *UWASISII: A Taxonomy of Social Goals and Human Service Programs.* Alexandria, VA: United Way of America, 1976.

Sunley, Robert. *Advocating Today: A Human Service Practitioner's Handbook.* New York: Family Service America, 1983.

Sun-Sentinel Editorial. "Drastic Reform Needed to Correct Long List of HRS Shortcomings." Ft. Lauderdale, FL: *Sun-Sentinel,* January 20, 1991, p. 4G.

Teigsler, K. "Evaluation of Education for Generalist Practice", *Journal of Education for Social Work.* Vol. 19, Winter 1983, pp. 79–85.

Toffler, Alvin. *Future Shock.* New York: Random House, 1970.

Toffler, Alvin. *Powershift.* New York: Bantam Books, 1990.

Tripodi, T. *Evaluative Research for Social Workers.* Englewood Cliffs, NJ: Prentice-Hall, 1983.

U.S. House of Representatives. *A Discursive Dictionary of Health Care.* Washington, DC: Government Printing Office, February, 1976.

Vigilante, Florence Wexler and Mildred D. Mailick. "Needs-Resource Evaluation in the Assessment Process," *Social Work,* March–April 1988, pp.-104.

Williams, George. "The Impact of Emerging Technology on Health Evaluation and Maintenance," in *Technology and Health Care Systems in the 1980s,* Morris Collen, (ed.). Washington, DC: U.S.D.H.E.W., 1972, Chapter 18, pp. 193–198.

Williamson, David G. *New Alliances in Health Care.* Richmond, VA: Medical College of Virginia, Virginia Commonwealth University, March 21, 1986.

Windsor, Richard, Thomas Baranowski, Noreen Clark, Gary Cutter. *Evaluation of Health Promotion and Education Programs.* Palo Alto, CA: Mayfield, 1984.

Zaldivar, R.A. "One-stop Shopping Idea Brings Many Social Services Under One Roof." Miami, FL: *The Miami Herald,* May 12, 1991, p. 13A.

Zaltman, Gerald and Brian Sternthal, (eds.). *Broadening the Concept of Consumer Behavior.* Association for Consumer Research, 1975.

PART IV

HUMAN SERVICES FOR THE FUTURE

In Part I of this volume, we examined the evolution of governmental, voluntary, and private HSOs in the 20th Century. In Part II, we examined human services trends and common human needs in the 1990s, as well as several recently-arrived HSOs, and their evolution. In Part III, we proposed the creation of the role of Human Services Worker, to fulfill a variety of functions, after appropriate education/training, in an attempt to better meet client needs and address some frequently-encountered areas of client dissatisfaction. In Part IV, we have attempted to identify several human service areas in which we expect pronounced movement during the coming decade, so that by the 21st Century, significant inroads will have been made in the provision of such services vis-a-vis their current status. It should be clear that these services do not necessarily represent *personal* choices/desires on the part of the authors, but rather are the result of our analysis of recent trends, future projections, various demographic factors, and the evolutionary process of human service organizations, as previously discussed. In other words, a variety of forces, presently observable, leads the authors to expect these human service areas to undergo considerable volatility as we approach the next millenium.

NATIONAL HEALTH INSURANCE

The first thing we need to do here is distinguish between "national health insurance" and "national health service." The terms are frequently interchanged in discussions and the literature, but in general, do *not* refer to the same concept. The term "national health insurance" (NHI), as used here, is more restrictive than the other, and while not yet precisely defined in the U.S., generally describes a uniform program of comprehensive health *financing*. "National health service" (NHS), on the other hand, usually refers to health programs in which the national government *directly operates* a health system to serve some or all its

93

citizens (Goldstein, 1989, p. 178; U.S. House of Representatives, February 1976, p. 106). Our focus here is on the former.

By focusing on NHI, which, as Weber contends, may only have a *major* impact on the ability to purchase services (Weber, 1972), we are not dismissing the problems surrounding other issues of concern regarding health care delivery in the U.S.—including distribution of services, accessibility, quality, etc. However, in this part of the book we are attempting to discuss arenas of human service in which we expect substantial movement in the 1990s. The political/economic climate of the U.S., discussed in Part II, would not lead us to believe there is enough widespread support, on all necessary levels, for a national health service in the near future. In regard to the issue of national health insurance, the climate appears quite different.

For those interested in the issue of national health services, we would refer you to the considerable body of work that exists—much of it completed by Milton Roemer (Roemer, 1976; Roemer, 1977a; Roemer, 1977b)—but also by others (DeMiguel, 1975; Terris, 1978; Elling, 1980; Raffel, 1984) interested in a cross-national comparison of health care systems. Paul Stuart has provided a related framework for a cross-national comparison of social welfare systems (Stuart, 1985) which also addresses concerns discussed in this volume, and Camp and Speidel have *combined* many of the variables studied by those who focus on *either* health or welfare problems, through the development of an "international human suffering index"—which incorporates measures of inflation, infant mortality, nutrition, adult literacy, and clean water, among others (Camp and Speidel, 1987). These are all appropriate sources for those who wish to examine further the issues of NHS.

In regard to NHI, however, its modern precedent lies in the health care, retirement systems, and other social programs begun in Bismarck's Germany in 1883. In the century since, most countries have developed some form of NHI, universal coverage, or comprehensive medical care (Balog, 1990).

Between 1916–1918, attempts were made by 16 state legislatures in America to establish some form of compulsory health insurance— essentially as a mechanism to help families pay for health services, which were already being felt as costly and often unpredictable. However, mass political support in the respective states was not present, and there was solid opposition from the American Medical Association, insurance companies, the pharmaceutical industry and businesses opposed to the imposition of payroll taxes. The supporters of such legislation—largely from the fields of labor economics, social work, and public health—had underestimated the strength of the opposition and overestimated the interest of middle-income Americans. As a result, the next significant development in health insurance was actually in the voluntary, not-for-profit sector, with the establishment of the Blue Cross plans, which grew out of a Baylor University Hospital Plan established in Dallas in 1929. This activity was the result of concern over high cost episodes of hospital care and depleted hospital financing—aggravated by the Great Depression (Anderson, 1975).

Starting in the 1930s, and continuing through the years of World War II, private insurance companies began to add health insurance coverage for hospital, surgical, and medical expenses to their accident and life insurance business. During World War II, when wages were frozen, group health insurance became an attractive fringe benefit for many workers. As a fringe benefit, it was not subjected to income or Social Security taxes. Soon, health insurance was a popular benefit in collective bargaining. In the early 1950s, insurers began to offer major medical expense insurance to cover catastrophic cases (Health Insurance Association of America, 1990).

After World War II, while countries such as the United Kingdom and Canada were accelerating activities in this area, now that resources were freed-up from the war effort, a National Health Insurance Plan was first proposed for the U.S. by President Truman, in 1948. The proposal was not politically viable at the time, and after years of effort by the Social Security Administration to develop health and disability insurance programs, and the enactment of the Kerr-Mills legislation, which provided medical assistance to elderly people on welfare or medically indigent, the groundwork was laid for the passage of Medicare in 1965 (Balog, 1990; Berkowitz, 1989).

Since the advent of Medicare—and Medicaid—in 1965 (the latter serving the indigent and medically indigent via shared federal/state programs), a variety of pressures/problems have evolved to help build the powerful constituency which will be needed to institutionalize NHI in this country. By the 1990s, a variety of data had evolved to provoke a number of serious proposals for NHI over the previous two decades. Precipitating factors (Eilers and Moyerman, 1971) included:

- A significant increase in health care costs.
- Dissatisfaction with current health delivery arrangements.

• Deficiencies in the private and social programs available for financing health care.

The 1987 National Medical Expenditure Survey (Short, Monheit and Beauregard, 1989) revealed that about 15 percent (37 million persons) of the total noninstitutionalized population in 1987 was uninsured for health care expenses. This figure is similar to that reported by the Health Insurance Association of America in 1988—that 13 percent of the civilian noninstitutionalized population lacked health care coverage (Health Insurance Association of America, 1990, p. 9). Gaps in insurance coverage were found primarily among:

—Young adults
—Blacks
—Hispanics
—The unmarried
—Families without a working adult
—Low wage/part-time workers
—The self-employed
—Workers in industries with second or temporary employment
—Employees of small firms

The Survey found that 25 percent of adult workers under 65 years of age and their families lacked work-related coverage through employers or unions. Most of the uninsured population under age 65 is, in fact, composed of workers and their families. Such workers tend to cluster in employment situations where the work is seasonal, temporary, involving low-level technical skills, sales, repairs, personal services, or self-employment. As one health economist has pointed out, poverty is closely related to the lack of health insurance, as large numbers of poor people are without coverage and/or served by inadequate Medicaid programs (Berki, 1990).

The consequences of being without health insurance include: being at significantly greater risk of having poor or fair health, than those with such insurance; lost opportunities to compete at school or work; and lack of significant preparation to mature into healthy adulthood without a host of chronic illnesses that result in a lifetime of dependency (Babcock, 1990; Davis and Rowland, 1990).

Shifts in the economy in the 1980s—especially the marked decline in heavy manufacturing—are expected to continue in the 1990s. Many of the affected industries are those which have been traditionally unionized, and have had well-established health plans. The expansion of service and retail jobs in their place expands the employment sector which has traditionally lacked adequate health insurance coverage for workers (Nexon, 1990). There are serious consequences of these shifts in the economy—not only for those currently employed, but also those who are retired. A recent National Medical Expenditure Survey of health insurance coverage among retired persons indicated that almost 50 percent of retired individuals depend upon employer-related retiree health benefits to supplement Medicare, and the present unfunded corporate liabilities for future retiree health benefits are causing considerable concern. To a lesser degree, private policies are purchased by 30 percent of retirees to supplement Medicare, and about 20 percent receive Medicaid or some other form of public medical assistance (Monheit and Schur, 1989).

The traditional antipathy toward NHI, on the part of some powerful elements in the U.S. has been weakening in recent years. While there is hardly a groundswell of support for a full-fledged NHS, three factors are significantly changing the debate over NHI (Albritton, 1990):

• The experience of some legislators who face constituents concerned over health care issues in their districts.

• The necessity for cost containment in meeting our deficit obligations.

• The changing orientation of the corporate business sector, which has been closely tied to the provision of increasingly-expensive health insurance benefits to employees.

The Robert Wood Johnson Foundation's Health Care for the Uninsured Program has been particularly concerned about the lack of a national solution to the growing problem of the uninsured. In view of the traditional lack of a national consensus on the issue, it has focused on state policy-makers through demonstration projects that serve as prominent examples of how the public and private sectors can collaborate in developing and implementing innovative financing and service delivery mechanisms to improve access for the uninsured. Operational projects, as of March 1, 1991, were located in the states of Arizona, Maine, Washington, Tennessee, Michigan, Wisconsin, Florida, Colorado, Utah and Alabama. In Florida, for example, the program—known as Florida Health Access—is a state-subsidized program of managed health care for small businesses, which operates in four service delivery areas, covering a total of thirteen counties. Over 1000 small firms are enrolled in the program, providing coverage to approximately 5000 workers and their dependents. Funds to support the program come from the state, the counties and the Robert Wood Johnson Foundation. These programs serve as an example of the current experimental attempts to grapple with one or more problematic areas among the uninsured (Alpha Center, April 1991).

In November 1989, Henry Ford Hospital organized its first urban health care symposium, "Urban Health Care: Solutions for the 1990s." Participants in the symposium agreed that new models of health care financing and delivery must be adopted in the 1990s, and a willingness to innovate and experiment should be encouraged. Concern was expressed not only for the millions of Americans without health insurance, but also for those with *inadequate* coverage—an even greater number (Benfer and Sahney, 1990). The greatest political drawbacks to the development of NHI were seen to be the federal deficit and failure to reach a consensus for action (Albritton, 1990). However, the recent passage and swift recision of the Medicare Catastrophic Coverage Act of 1988—which reduced out-of-pocket health care costs for many noninstitutionalized elderly, may have made some legislators wary of any changes which might anger the powerful seniors lobby. The latter mounted an effective vocal grassroots campaign to rescind this legislation, as too many middle-income retirees resented the increased deductibles they encountered under it, in order to subsidize the poorer elderly sector. The country's experience with this failed program may suggest that the direction should be to make broader legislative changes—affecting all or most of the population—rather than limited segments (Monheit and Schur, 1989).

At any rate, the past two decades have witnessed a plethora of NHI proposals in the U.S. While there can be considerable variation from one proposal to another, generally the objectives of an NHI program include (Weber, 1972):

• The provision of protection against high-cost illness.

• An increase in equity, or reduction of inequality, in the receipt of care.

• Restraining the rate of growth in per unit cost of health care.

• Increasing the production of preventive medicine and early diagnostic services.

The well-articulated proposal for NHI usually includes a discussion of (Weber, 1972):

• The population to be covered (eligibility).

• The services to be covered.

• Comprehensiveness of care.

- Who pays for services, and how?
- How will institutions/providers be reimbursed?

More recent proposals have also included, in addition to the above, a discussion of:

- Cost control.
- Consumer participation and control.
- Quality control.
- Research and demonstration programs.

Cost control has been addressed by the proposals for NHI in a variety of ways. Some proposals have focused on "catastrophic health insurance," usually defined as protection against the high cost of treating *severe* or *lengthy* illnesses or disabilities. Generally such proposals cover all or a specified percentage of medical expenses above an amount that is the responsibility of the insured (Goldstein, 1989, pp. 40–41; U.S. House of Representatives, February 1976, p. 24). Most proposals attempt to control costs through such provisions as (Balog, 1990):

- Copayments (the patient pays *something* for all or most services).
- Deductibles (plan coverage begins only after the patient has incurred some minimum of personal cost each year).
- Spending caps (the government pays only a certain amount per patient in each time period).
- Regulated provider fees (hospital and physician fees are preset and increases are regulated).
- Queuing (health services are rationed by assigning priorities for type of procedure, patient's age, or other criteria).

Anderson reports that the Blue Cross Plans assume NHI will bring additional pressures to hold down health care costs, through greater cost containment—as well as better utilization review, planning, increased efficiency, and public accountability (Anderson, 1975).

Another area of differentiation among NHI plans often involves the extent to which the federal government shares the cost of the program with the states (similar to the basis of Medicaid financing), versus, for example, a more revolutionary approach which involves the adoption of a system of compulsory health insurance, funded through general tax revenues or special taxes (Bachman and Meriam, 1976).

Perhaps the most striking thing one observes in perusing proposals for NHI, formulated in the past several decades, is the wide variety of sponsors. A selective, nonexhaustive list of such proposals includes

(Eilers and Moyerman, 1971; Waldman, 1976; Pepper Commission, September 1990 b; Moss, February, 1991):

- Medicredit (American Medical Association)
- Aetna Plan (Aetna Life and Casualty Company)
- Rockefeller Plan (Governor Nelson Rockefeller)
- Feldstein Plan (Martin S. Feldstein, Health Economist)
- Javits Plan (Senator Jacob Javits)
- Griffiths Plan (Congresswoman Martha Griffiths)
- Kennedy Plan (Committee for National Health Insurance)
- HIAA Plan (Health Insurance Association of America)
- Ameriplan (American Hospital Association)
- Nixon Plan for NHI (President Richard M. Nixon)
- National Leadership Commission Plan
- A Consumer-Choice Health Plan for the 1990s
- Physicians for a National Health Policy
- NASW National Health Care Plan (National Association of Social Workers)
- Basic Health Benefits for All Americans Act (Senator Kennedy/ Representative Waxman)

One can see from the above, selective, partial list, that "everyone has been getting into the act." Proposals have come from the political sector (presidents, governors, members of Congress); from professional associations (American Medical Association, American Hospital Association, National Association of Social Workers, Physicians for a National Health Policy); the insurance industry (Aetna, Health Insurance Association of America); academics (Martin Feldstein); and broad-based consumer-oriented groups (Committee for National Health Insurance).

By way of example, we shall discuss but one of the above proposals — the recent Basic Health Benefits for All Americans Act — BHB (Senate Bill S.768, November 20, 1989). Senator Ted Kennedy, the Senate sponsor, has been associated with a variety of bills for some years, revising/refining them to ultimately arrive at a form that is likely to be acceptable on the political level. His latest effort consists of two major packages — an employer package and a public package — each of which is summarized below (Senate Bill S. 768, November 20, 1989; Nexon, 1990; Federation of American Health Systems Review, 1990; Pepper Commission, September 1990a; Pepper Commission, September 1990b):

The Employer Package: This package requires employers to provide a basic package of health benefits to all full-time employees and their dependents. It would encompass 23 million (two-thirds) of those currently uninsured. The basic package would include physician and hospital services, diagnostic tests, prenatal and well-baby care, limited mental health benefits, and catastrophic coverage (defined as uncovered costs above $3000). There are maximum limits on deductibles, copayments and the employer's share of the premiums. *No one can be excluded from coverage for reasons of health status or preexisting conditions.* Because of the unique problems of employers with small numbers of employees, there are special conditions where 25 or less employees are on the payroll. In order for a company to sell health insurance to such employers, it must be first certified by the federal government—a process that requires a commitment to accept any small business that applies for coverage for its employees; a commitment to offer community-rated coverage; and a commitment not to reject any applicant on the basis of health status. A subsidy would be offered to small businesses for which the cost of compliance with the law would be excessive.

The Public Package: This package represents a federal/state program, similar to Medicaid, which would be phased in, for purposes of political expediency, as follows:

Phase 1:   All uninsured children below 185 percent of the poverty level and pregnant women between 100–185 percent of the poverty level would be covered (pregnant women below 100% of the poverty level are already covered through existing programs). These provisions would cover 4 million people, and it is believed by the sponsors that this can be accomplished with relatively low initial federal cost.

Phase 2:   In 1996, the remaining uninsured would be covered— those who are not children or pregnant women, and those with income between 100–185 percent of the poverty level. This would add 5.7 million people.

Phase 3:   In 1999, the federal government would assume coverage for every other uninsured American.

Sponsors of BHB believe it is the best current alternative from among the proposals being presented because: (1) a full-blown European-style NHS is too radical an idea for the U.S. at this time; (2) expansion of Medicaid to include everyone without employment-based insurance (including those who are employed) would be too expensive and weaken the employment-based precedent; and (3) BHB reinforces the importance of coverage for *all* workers and dependents through employment, and only involves the public sector in those cases where a person is ineligible for employment-based coverage.

Doubtless, there will be additional proposals for NHI made in the 1990s. When one examines the evolutionary process for new human services discussed in Part II, there is reason to believe that before this decade is over, the U.S. will have instituted some form of NHI. As the above discussion about uninsured/underinsured citizens indicates, the problem is no longer viewed as an individual one; the problem has received considerable media attention; a variety of solutions have been suggested; statistical data and research findings have accumulated to underpin the debate; and governmental bodies at both the federal and state levels have attempted to address the issue.

SERVICES FOR THE HOMELESS

The first difficulty one encounters in discussing services for the "homeless" is in defining the term. Despite considerable recent media attention to the problem, there is no agreed-upon definition. This obviously affects any count of the homeless one might report.

The Federal Department of Housing and Urban Development established a definition in 1984 to which many, but not all, subscribe. In their definition, a homeless person is one who spends the night in a public or private emergency shelter or receives temporary vouchers for shelter, or spends the night in spaces not designed for shelter—such as the streets (U.S. Department of Housing and Urban Development, 1984, p. 291).

Even with such a broad definition, Applebaum points out that the actual count of the number of homeless is subject to considerable question regarding validity and reliability. Persons questioned about their homeless status may not be entirely honest for a variety of reasons, they may refuse to answer at all, and they may even not all be accessible to researchers. Thus, he expects the result will always be an *undercount,* and as such, may be counterproductive when social programs and legislative remedies are based on such counts (Applebaum, 1990). As a result of the multiple definitions of homelessness, and the problems of counting persons in such a state, it is not surprising that national estimates vary widely, ranging from a low of 250,000 to a high of 3 million. This inherent problem also affects attempts to determine the characteristics of the homeless, and the causes of the problem (Hopps, 1989).

Homeless persons who use services such as shelters are obviously more accessible to study than those who do not. A national, representative sample of over 1700 such individuals yielded the following sociodemographic profile (Burt and Cohen, 1990):

- The adult homeless population is predominantly male (81%).
- More than 50 percent of shelter users are black or Hispanic.
- Families comprise 10 percent of those who use shelters.
- Shelter users tend to be less well-educated than the general U.S. population.
- Many shelter users fall in the 24–44 age group.
- Most shelter users are single.
- Most shelter users are residents of the host-city (not outsiders).
- Persons in shelters tend to lack the job skills needed to get back into the mainstream.
- Respondents reported receiving very little cash within the 30-day period prior to being interviewed. If they were female, they were more likely to have income from means-tested programs.
- The median length of time respondents reported being homeless was 10 months. However, the average was 39 months, a figure skewed by a small number of cases in the sample with an extremely long period of homelessness—in some cases more than 10 years (service providers generally believe that the length of time someone has been homeless is a rough indicator of how difficult it will be to help that person resume a stable life in the community).
- Those most likely to be receiving public benefits have a history of mental hospitalization, chemical dependency, or dependent children.
- 19 percent had spent at least one night in a mental hospital at some point in their lives.
- 33 percent had been patients in a detoxification or treatment center for alcohol/drug abuse.
- 52 percent had spent time in a city or county jail.
- 24 percent had been in state or federal prisons.

Burt and Cohen determined that shelters are not the ultimate solution, but a humane and essential first response. They suggest that policymakers need to look at the complex shifts and changes that have occurred during the decade of the 1980s in the housing market, job market, in the buying power of housing support and income support programs, in eligibility for public support programs, in the buying power of the minimum wage, and in the skill levels of the labor force. The increasing "affordable housing gap" in many communities makes it less likely that poor people, including those with disabilities, can afford housing. They conclude that no single, simple approach will address this complex problem—because the homeless population itself includes people who have become homeless for different reasons and in different ways. They suggest a multifaceted approach will be needed.

In Part I of this book, we discussed the three categories of human services—governmental, voluntary, private. In regard to services for the homeless, the field is limited to governmental programs and those offered by the voluntary not-for-profit sector.

On the national level, the federal government became concerned about the homeless in 1967, when Congress amended Title I of the Social Security Act to establish the Emergency Assistance Program (EA), as a component to Aid to Dependent Children (AFDC)—to aid homeless families. In a Congressional review conducted some years later (1986) the Committee on Governmental Operations of the House criticized the EA program as unable to address the problems of homeless families. The Committee charged that the Department of Health and Human Services (HHS) had failed to follow its own regulations on monitoring, reviewing, and auditing such programs. It also determined that the shelter system was destructive to families, harmful to children, and may be actually perpetuating long-term homelessness among families. It suggested HHS better regulate and review EA programs, use EA funds in conjunction with state and local governments to develop a model shelter program for the homeless, and that the President should issue an Executive Order declaring homelessness a national emergency and require the federal government to coordinate all existing resources (U.S. House of Representatives, October 9, 1986).

Several additional federal initiatives have been the establishment of a clearinghouse on homelessness among mentally ill people, by the National Institutes of Mental Health and the Alcohol, Drug Abuse and Mental Health Administration—and the passage of the Stewart B. McKinney Homeless Relief Act, in 1987 (Daly, 1990).

The McKinney Act (Public Law 100-77) was signed into law on July 22, 1987. It has been amended as recently as 1990 (U.S. Congress, July 10, 1990). The Act authorizes money for housing, health, community services, education, and nutrition programs for the homeless. Its recognition of the multifaceted nature of the problem is owed, in part, to hearings previously held in the U.S. Congress in the early 1980s, when the Subcommittee on Housing and Community Development of the House of Representatives became the first body of Congress to explore and bring into public view the problems of the homeless (U.S. House of Representatives, January 25, 1984).

In addition to such federal initiatives, there has been involvement at the state levels. In a recent report to the governor of Florida, for example (Department of Health and Rehabilitative Services, June 30, 1990), surveys indicate there are between 17,000–28,000 homeless people on any given day in Florida (the wide variation is due to pronounced seasonal fluctuations due to the State's attractive climate in winter). Characteristics of the Florida homeless include the following (categories are not mutually exclusive):

- 37 percent are families.
- 20 percent are children and/or runaway youths.
- 70 percent are "new" homeless.
- 30 percent are chronic homeless and traditional street people.
- 60 percent are Florida residents.
- 30 percent suffer from mental illness, alcoholism, or chemical dependency, or other health problems.
- Approximately 15 percent are displaced farm workers, refugees, veterans, deinstitutionalized mentally ill, or those released from jails and prisons.

Studies in Florida indicate that the major causes of homelessness there are consistent with national trends (Department of Health and Rehabilitative Services, June 30, 1990):

- Lack of affordable housing.
- Unemployment and poor wages.
- Family disintegration.
- Poverty.
- Lack of education/training.
- Alcohol/chemical dependency.
- Mental illness.
- Migration.
- Immigration.
- Free will.

Florida has focused on two major initiatives in regard to the homeless: (1) prevention and early intervention; and (2) actions to reduce and alleviate homeless conditions when and where they occur. Specific programs have included (Department of Health and Rehabilitative Services, June 30, 1990):

• An emergency financial assistance program designed to provide a one-time $400 grant to homeless families and those at immediate risk of homelessness due to eviction, loss of wages, and other conditions that cause sudden economic deprivation.

• The 1990 Session of the Florida legislature appropriated $15 million to the Department of Community Affairs for affordable housing.

• The Florida legislature has authorized a grant-in-aid program to assist community agencies and organizations serving the homeless— including local homeless coalitions.

• There are 22 state-funded domestic violence centers, without which perhaps thousands of abused women and their children would be homeless and on the streets.

• There is a statewide network of 25 homeless youth shelters.

• Through the Department of Health and Rehabilitative Services, county public health units provide free medical care to Florida's homeless.

• A variety of other state programs—such as employment and training, child support enforcement, Aid to Families with Dependent Children, food stamps, and Medicaid help ensure minimum income levels necessary to the avoidance of economic destitution and homelessness.

Concern for the homeless at the local level was repeatedly stressed by the U.S. Conference of Mayors during the 1980s (U.S. Conference of Mayors, 1986; U.S. Conference of Mayors, 1987; U.S. Conference of Mayors, December 1987). In fact, the local level became directly involved with the problem long before the federal and state governments. On the local level, the homeless have been assisted for over 100 years, by a combination of local government and local organizations/agencies/charities. Currently, 70 percent or more of all emergency services in Florida are rendered by local agencies with grassroots financial support. This results in the generation of 3500 emergency shelter beds out of a total of 4500 statewide, via local efforts. While such local initiatives have tended to concentrate on emergency needs—such as shelter, food, clothing, medical care, money, work, counseling, detoxification, spiritual counseling, and sometimes housing—they have lately become concerned with a broader range of homeless needs. The latter include case management, assistance in locating permanent housing, assistance in obtaining permanent employment, transportation, child day care, alcohol/drug abuse treatment, mental health treatment, rent subsidies, rent supplements, security deposits, utility connections, family shelter, transitional housing, and prevention (Department of Health and Rehabilitative Services, June 30, 1990).

The emphasis on emergency shelter care, which predominates at the local level, doesn't always distinguish among the homeless—who have varying needs. Buss believes that we must recognize the fact that the homeless often need assistance beyond temporary, emergency shelter, when public policy is being developed. He identifies three distinct groups (Buss, 1990):

• People who are unlikely to function outside a protected environment (those in need of permanent custodial care).

• Homeless persons who are unable to achieve economic self-sufficiency because of a major deficit (such as illiteracy) or a chronic problem (such as alcoholism) with which they cannot cope unaided.

• Homeless individuals or families in crisis for a variety of reasons (in need of short-term crisis care—counseling, financial support, etc.).

In his discussion of public policy and the homeless, Buss favors a two-pronged approach: (1) preventing some people from becoming homeless in the first place; and (2) fostering the reintegration of some homeless with society and providing permanent custodial care for others. He is opposed to wholesale forced sheltering (which may interfere with constitutional rights), massive reinstitutionalization of the mentally ill, and encouragement of the homeless to live in jerry-built shacks, squatter-style (Buss, 1990).

One of the most comprehensive local efforts to study the problems of the homeless in the United States, to date, is the Barry University Study, supported by the Posner Fund, and conducted in South Florida in the winter of 1989—in cooperation with Florida International University, Florida Atlantic University, and the University of Miami. Its primary findings were (Fike, 1988; Dluhy, 1991):

• About 25 percent of the homeless are *situationally* homeless (on the street for the first time, remaining there not more than 90 days, and needing immediate assistance to get back on their feet).

• About 30 percent are *episodic* homeless (moving in and out of housing and the economy, with each episode becoming longer and longer. Some may have intermittent problems with substance abuse and mental illness, but their problems are, for the most part, treatable).

• About 30 percent are *chronic* homeless (usually severely mentally ill, chronic substance abusers, or have a dual diagnosis of both problems.

They have been on the street a long time, perhaps years, and need managed care and supervision).

• About 15 percent are *street people* (persons who have "dropped out", eschewed the work ethic and freely chosen to avoid work, bills, family and even permanent relationships. They often avoid programs for the homeless, except shelters, and indicate they don't want rehabilitation).

Recommendations from the Barry University Study, for handling the homeless problem in South Florida, include (Dluhy, 1991):

• Development of a centralized assessment and receiving center that diagnoses the problems of the homeless, then places them in appropriate settings. Ideally, case managers would follow-up on them, perhaps for several years.

• Establish a nonprofit housing corporation to build and manage 60 facilities of approximately 30 units each to house the most severely mentally and physically disabled.

• Organize a housing voucher and placement program to locate low-cost permanent housing, and subsidize this housing until occupants can pay for it themselves, or until they qualify to receive government benefits.

• Design and fund preventive programs that identify and help "at risk" families and children who are one step from homelessness and the degrading experience of street life.

• Use local resources to start up "self-help" businesses and industries run by the homeless themselves.

• Set up a coordinating council of community leaders from all the county's major sectors to make sure the plan is implemented.

In addition to the foregoing examples of governmental involvement with the problems of the homeless, an example from the voluntary, not-for-profit sector is the National Health Care for the Homeless Program, funded by the Robert Wood Johnson Foundation and the Pew Charitable Trust. Under this program, 220,000 homeless persons were examined at shelter clinics in 19 cities across the U.S. between 1985–1989, and the results have recently been published in a single volume (Brickner, 1990).

While much attention in research has been directed toward identifying the homeless and assessing their problems, Hagen and Hutchison have asked a collateral question of importance—*who* is serving the homeless? In a survey conducted among 71 providers of service in 15 agencies, they found that the staff in voluntary agencies have been in the vanguard of services to the homeless—particularly in providing emergency shelter, soup kitchens and food pantries, followed by the later entrance of public agencies. In the sample studied, the "typical" provider of services to the homeless was a white female, average age of 33.8 years, earning an income which ranged from $10,000–$30,000 per year. These providers had widely-different educational backgrounds, but only 10 percent had a BSW and 18 percent had an MSW—thus only slightly more than one-quarter had educational preparation in social work at either the undergraduate or graduate levels. Almost half had been in their current positions less than one year, with the average length of time in current positions being 16 months. They worked primarily in shelters, where they had been successful in negotiating income maintenance and mental health services for clients, but less successful in gaining access to permanent housing. Because of the degree of mental illness encountered, as well as suicide attempts among clients, Hagen and Hutchison recommend that extensive knowledge of human behavior and intervention strategies should be an important part of the training of such individuals. The need for a broad-based professional human services curriculum is implied in the wide-ranging functions performed by this group, including concrete services (food, short-term housing); information on services; advocacy; referral; intervention and diagnosis; counseling; and case management (Hagen and Hutchison, 1988).

In summary, our current understanding of the "homeless problem" indicates it is a multidimensional, multicausal problem. Some of the causes are external to the homeless person, some internal, and some the result of the interaction of the individual with his/her environment. In view of these research findings, the homeless population will have to be diagnosed and segmented and appropriate solutions applied on an individual basis, if necessary, rather than solely on a global, macrobasis. The problem of the homeless has received considerable attention in the media during the past decade. Activists such as the late Mitch Snyder of the Community for Creative Nonviolence (Momeni, 1990, p. 170), who was able to attract show business celebrities to the cause, have made the problem highly visible in the media, as well as on many big-city streets. And former U.S. President Jimmy Carter, and his wife, Rosalynn, have garnered considerable publicity for Habitat for Humanity, a Christian organization which has built about 10,000 basic homes since its founding 15 years ago, and to which the Carters personally donate time from their busy schedules (Habitat for Humanity, 1991).

However, as the research of Hagen and Hutchison, cited above, indicates, a systems approach to helping the homeless will be necessary (Thorman,

1988). Well-trained providers, with a multiplicity of skills, will be needed to steer the homeless through the maze of federal, state, and local programs—both governmental and voluntary—and to coordinate (case manage) the services until the client can once more be independent. If ever there were a client population for whom the new Human Services Worker described in Part III of this book were appropriate, it would appear to be the homeless client. Both the proposed training for HSWs, and the proposed functions of assessment, referral, client advocacy, coordination and evaluation, would allow them to make meaningful contributions in addressing this complex problem and its segmented client population.

Using the evolutionary scheme for HSOs presented in Part II of this volume, the problem of the homeless has moved from a low profile, individual issue to one of greater visibility—in part due to media attention and in part due to sheer numbers of people living on the street. Pioneering solutions, usually of a voluntary nature at the local level, have been tried, while statistical data and research findings have accumulated to motivate governmental bodies to initiate legislative remedies. We expect this process to continue, and accelerate, during the 1990s.

DAY CARE FOR CHILDREN

Like most other concepts in the human services area, "day care" has been variously defined. The definition provided by Marver and Larson— that day care is any kind of regular supervision of a child, when he/she is not in school, provided by anyone other than the child's parents— is broad enough to suit our purposes in this discussion (Marver and Larson, 1978).

According to Clarke-Stewart (Clarke-Stewart, 1982), day care has a long history in the United States, precipitated by the flood of immigrants between the years 1815–1860, and the rapid industrialization and urbanization of the time—which took women out of their homes and into factories. Concern over unattended children of working mothers prompted intervention by wealthy women and service organizations concerned over the resultant neglect, lack of sanitation, and vice. The first American day nursery is believed to have opened in Boston in 1838 to provide care for the children of seamen's working wives and widows. Later, similar facilities were opened in New York City, Philadelphia, and Chicago. By 1898, 175 day nurseries were operating around the country, most often set up in converted homes. The focus of care tended to be "custodial"—with an emphasis on basic health and safety, and it was considered somewhat of a last resort for children who couldn't be cared for at home. Because so many of these children were the offspring of immigrants, some of the day care facilities offered instruction on American manners and hygiene in addition to the custodial supervision.

A major advancement occurred in 1933 when federal funds for the expansion of day care first became available under the Federal Economic Recovery Act and the Works Project Administration (WPA) initiated by President Franklin Roosevelt. These funds helped create jobs for unemployed teachers, nurses, cooks, and janitors—occupations which lent their skills to day care. By 1937, these programs had set up 1900 day nurseries, caring for 40,000 children. With the decline of the WPA in 1938, day care also declined—until World War II. Due to the mass mobilization of women into war-related industries, and renewed financial support provided by the Lanham Act in 1942, prejudice against working women subsided and day care flourished. By 1945, over one and one-half million children were in day care—where many of the centers were of an "innovative" nature—sometimes offering shopping and medical services, as well as carry-out dinners for busy mothers (Clarke-Stewart, 1982).

Many centers closed after World War II, when the Lanham funds were withdrawn in 1946. From 1950–1965 day care was, once again, a marginal service for the poor, with an emphasis on "problem families." But, women continued to work anyway, using a variety of arrangements—relatives, neighbors, housekeepers—if they weren't poor enough to qualify for public-supported day care. In the mid-1960s, attitudes toward day care began to become more positive as it was recognized that many mothers were now in the labor force, and day care provisions would allow more women to get off welfare. Federal support became available again, though still only for poor families. A milestone occurred in 1965 with Project Head Start, a national program which provided nursery-school education for poor children. While it was only a part-day program—offering limited help to mothers working full-time—it did focus public attention on the idea that education was important for all young children, not just those from affluent families. As a result, middle-class parents and women's groups pressed for educational day care programs, and as a consequence, public monies were made available through a variety of federal programs in the late 1960s (Clarke-Stewart, 1982).

At the 1970 White House Conference on Children, day care was selected as the most serious problem confronting American families and children. Since that time, numerous day care-related bills have been presented in Congress each session. A major federal involvement occurred in 1974 when Title XX of the Social Security Act was amended (Public Law 93-647, October 1, 1975) to allow additional federal subsidies for day care for the poor. Other federal programs with day care components include the Comprehensive Employment and Training Act (CETA), Federal Employment Assistance Program for Native Americans (regulated by the Bureau of Indian Affairs), the aforementioned Head Start Program, and Aid to Families of Dependent Children—AFDC (Marver and Larson, 1978).

In the past several decades, considerable prominence has been given to day care as a national issue. As far back as 1960, the Child Welfare League of America published standards for day care (Child Welfare League of America, 1969)—but it wasn't until 1980 that the U.S. government, after much debate, established government standards for federally-supported day care—known as the Federal Interagency Day Care Requirements—FIDCR (Clarke-Stewart, 1982, p. 126). The National Organization for Women (NOW) included a demand for tax deductions for child care expenses for working parents in its Bill of Rights in 1969, along with establishment of child care centers, by law, on the same basis as parks, libraries, public schools, etc. And the National Women's Political Caucus Platform also demanded the passage of comprehensive child care legislation and an extension of temporary disability benefits to cover pregnancy, child birth, miscarriage, abortion, and recovery (Sochen, 1974, pp. 435–438).

There are a variety of forces pushing for further development of day care services and financing at this time in the United States. They include (Clarke-Stewart, 1982; Thorman, 1989):

• The fact that a majority of school-age children have working mothers.
• The prevalence of divorce.
• The prevalence of single parenthood.
• The supplanting of the extended family of the past by the nuclear family.
• Changes in social values—including the right of parents to develop their individual potential.
• The demands of the Women's Movement.
• Economic factors which require two-income families for a satisfactory standard of living.

A variety of day care forms have resulted from the above-mentioned forces. They include (Ainslie, 1984; Martin, 1990):

• In-house sitters (an adult comes to the home and watches the children who reside there. Working parents claim to prefer this, and especially like it for preschoolers. The sitter may be a relative or nonrelative, and may be paid or unpaid).

• Day care homes (the child goes to the sitter's house for supervision while his/her mother is at work).

• Nursery schools (child-oriented, center-based programs for preschoolers).

• Day care centers (which are similar to nursery schools, except they usually offer a longer day-of-care)

Sponsorship of day care, in its various forms, differs also, to include (Maynard, 1985; Thorman, 1989):

• Not-for-profit, voluntary, community care.

• Government-sponsored care (federal, state, local).

• Employer-sponsored care.

• For-profit, commercial care (about 60% of the total and the fastest growing sector).

• Church-sponsored care.

• Cooperative centers (where parents who usually work part-time and have flexible schedules share the workload).

• University/college-sponsored care.

• Day care in public schools.

A number of issues have arisen as a result of the prevalence and variety of day care, including:

• Issues of quality and standards, including what should be the standards and how should they be enforced (Child Welfare League of America, 1969; Sochen, 1974, pp. 435–438; Clarke-Stewart, 1982, p. 126).

• Issues of health and safety, ranging from questions over the direct provision of health services, such as immunizations and vision screening (Bowen, 1982) to concerns over the possibility of epidemics at the service site (Corpus and Corpus, 1991).

• Issues of legal obligation, resulting from the principle of "in loco parentis" (Blum, 1983, pp. 41–52). What liability does the caregiver incur in this capacity? For example, is the caregiver obligated/required to report suspected parental child abuse to authorities? (Streets, 1982).

• To what extent should medically at-risk children—such as those with cerebral palsy, ostomies, catheters, spina bifida, etc.—be accommodated, either in specialized centers or intermingled with well children? The Robert Wood Johnson Foundation is currently underwriting demonstration projects for services to such children in order to better understand the problems involved (Robert Wood Johnson Foundation, 1990).

• To what extent is a code of ethics needed, delineating appropriate behavior in day care settings toward parents, children, staff, and colleagues? (Katz, 1982).

• To what extent should staff be prepared, certified, and/or licensed for such a job, assisted with stress and burnout, provided with continuing education/training, and better compensated? (Whitebook et al., 1981).

• To what extent should care be of a *custodial,* supervisory nature versus *developmental,* i.e. providing for the child's social, emotional and educational growth? (Marver and Larson, 1978).

• To what extent does the proliferation of day care diminish the family and weaken it, as some believe (Hatch, 1982) versus the counterargument that affordable day care strengthens families on a number of levels (Kennedy, 1982).

• To what extent should the government, at all levels, become involved in the sponsorship/funding/provision of day care? (Kahn and Kamerman, 1987).

While all the above are worthy of further discussion, we shall focus on the last point, regarding governmental involvement in day care—both because of space limitations and the plethora of material available on the subject.

Our concern with day care in the United States has been cyclical, as the brief history cited above indicates. In times of war, it is highly regarded—and funds, including direct government subsidies, become available or increase. In times of postwar prosperity, it has been looked upon as a social stigma, and federal support, in particular, has decreased (Marver and Larson, 1978).

National attention has also been cyclical because of differing philosphies in the White House, as presidential administrations change. President Johnson, for instance, saw concerns for day care as part of the overall War on Poverty of the Great Society. President Nixon saw anything that encouraged women to leave the home as destructive of family life and family values (Thorman, 1989). Much of the debate between those with such opposing views on this subject (and other social issues) can be laid to a difference between a "normative" and "behaviorist" approach to life and its problems. In the normative approach, an "ideal" American family is postulated, with a father as breadwinner, mother as homemaker, and children. Social programs which make it possible for the mother to leave home, for work or self-fulfillment, while her young children are supervised by others, are seen as "destructive." In the behaviorist approach, proponents accept the fact that most families cannot live solely on a father's income anymore (even if he resides with the family—which is not always the case), that many women *are* working, and *will* work— regardless of the obstacles encountered—and the provision of affordable, safe day care for youngsters will keep the family intact and strengthen it. This difference in perspective, between "what should be" and "what is" underlies many social countroversies in this country.

Because of former President Reagan's political views in general, and inclinations toward the normative view on social matters, his administration emphasized decentralization, deregulation, and privatization of day care in establishing and implementing federal policy in the 1980s. With the transformation of Title XX into the Social Services Block Grant, all constraints on how funds were to be spent, and by whom, were eliminated. In addition, the elimination, or bypassing, of the aforementioned Federal Interagency Day Care Requirements left child care providers subject only to state standards of quality. Federal involvement in day care in recent years has thus emphasized (Kahn and Kamerman, 1987):

- Tax credits for parents who incur day care expense.
- Tax incentives for employers who provide day care services.

Kahn and Kamerman go on to explain that the consequences of the above approach have been: an increase in the diversity of day care services available; a decline in standards; and reduced subsidies for low-income children. Among the employer-supported services encouraged by this approach, they identify: paying for information and referral services for employees; obtaining discounts—often from large for-profit chains—for employees who use the chains' services; and providing on-site care for the children of employees—with hospitals dominating in the offering of such services to employees (Kahn and Kamerman, 1987).

Still, demand for day care exceeds supply, and one recent estimate projects that "approved" centers can only accommodate 1.5 million of the more than 7 million children in need of such care. The consequence is that some parents who could work, may not go to work at all; others may quit their jobs; others may leave their children in risky situations (Karger and Stoesz, 1990, p. 238); and long waiting lists will exist at many centers (Thorman, 1989, pp. 3–6). Beck is pessimistic about such movement on the federal level, as she views children's issues as rarely generating large numbers of votes or campaign funds in this country (Beck, 1982).

On the *state* level, variation is considerable. States differ on whether they have licensing requirements or not, on the required ratio of adults-to-infants, on the presence of mandatory staff training, and related issues (Thorman, 1989, p. 7). In this regard, the Florida legislature, for example, is currently considering a bill that would create statewide licensing and regulation of child care in private homes—currently limited to commercial day care centers. Proponents argue that for the first time, there will be minimum standards for all children in day care in the state. Certain national organizations, however, will be exempt. The bill also would increase one-time training and educational requirements for licensed child-care personnel from 20 hours to 30 hours, set specific staff ratios, set minimum space requirements, and require hospitals to distribute day care brochures upon the birth or adoption of a child and require that child care facilities provide information about themselves to the statewide child care resource and referral agencies. Federal funds would be used to hire additional inspectors needed under such a program (McGarrahan, 1991).

The above legislative proposal in Florida is an example of the fact that states are likely to become involved in, and expand, day care—if federal funds are made available. This has been at the heart of many congressional proposals in recent years, including the bill proposed in the late 1980s by Senator Christopher Dodd of Connecticut—the Act for Better Child Care Services. Under this bill, states could use federal funds to provide day care programs that are approved by the federal government and run by licensed practitioners. Parents with a family income less than 115 percent of the median for their respective state would be eligible for the subsidized programs (Thorman, 1989, p. 11).

Some other examples of state programs include (Thorman, 1989, p. 104):

• A program in Florida that lets employers deduct 100 percent of the start-up costs of an on-site child care center from state tax obligations.

• A Connecticut program which permits a 50 percent state tax credit for firms that offer their employees subsidies for child care, and grants corporations credit up to 40 percent for contributions to not-for-profit day care centers.

• Programs in over 50 percent of the states which provide income-tax credits to families for child care expenses, ranging from 10 percent of the federal credit in Arkansas to 45 percent in Iowa.

On the *local* level, a variety of programs exist, and once again, the situation varies from state-to-state, and *within* a given state. In Florida, for example, some counties have created their own licensing and rules for day care homes, despite the absence of statewide requirements, or requirements in neighboring counties (McGarrahan, 1991). And Thorman reports that some municipalities are using zoning ordinances to increase the number of day care facilities, by giving priority consideration to developers who include a day care center in commercial complexes they propose to build (Thorman, 1989, p. 104).

One might well ask where does all this leave us as we enter the last decade of the 20th Century? If one considers the evolutionary process for HSOs, discussed in Part II of this volume, one can clearly see that the problem no longer can be viewed as an individual one—too many children, in need of care, have working parents. The problem is also no longer a low-profile one—the media devote considerable attention to it. "Pioneering" solutions have been tried for decades—on the federal, state, and local levels—and of a for-profit, not-for-profit and cooperative nature. These efforts continue, such as the aforementioned demonstration projects of the Robert Wood Johnson Foundation (Robert Wood Johnson Foundation, 1990). Voluminous data have been collected by the Bureau of Labor Statistics, women's groups, educational groups, and others, and considerable research has been conducted on many different aspects of day care—cost, quality, licensing, staffing problems, etc. (the references cited in writing this section of the book provide further information of all these issues). And lastly, there has been a series of legislative actions on the federal and state levels, as well as through local ordinances, to deal with various aspects of the day care dilemma. The results of this lengthy process seem to be a rather widely-accepted consensus that enough material has been written and researched regarding day care so that it is now possible to articulate "ideal" guidelines. These include the notions that (Steinfels, 1973; Zigler and Gordon, 1982; Beck, 1982; Auerbach, 1979; Heller, 1982):

• Day care should be a national issue of concern to all, with a legitimate role for public support.

• Day care should take a holistic view toward the child and family/community of which he/she is a part.

• Coordination of day care services is necessary—preferably by municipal offices of child services.

• Appropriate health care services should be provided at day care centers.

• Bilingual/bicultural programs should be promoted in day care centers, where appropriate.

• Developmentally-disabled children should be included in day care centers.

• Expansion of current after-school programs should occur by providing a comprehensive before-and-after school service in every school.

• Day care is a necessity for children from all socioeconomic classes.

• Day care and the future of the family are linked together, thus parents should have a role in program development and policy-making.

• Day care should not be expanded so rapidly that quality suffers.

• Experimentation with different models should be encouraged, in order to create a system with sufficient flexibility to meet a variety of needs.

• Day care should be more than custodial—it must also be educational and developmental.

• Quality of care is very uneven, and minimum standards should be established everywhere necessary, and enforced.

As a result of our discussion of the political/economic/social trends projected for the 1990s (discussed in Part II) we do not foresee nationalized, federally-operated day care centers in the coming decade in the U.S.—except perhaps on a limited, experimental basis. The mix of for-profit, not-for-profit, multiple-sponsored services is expected to continue. It appears that continued growth will occur along the two primary vectors at which the day care movement has arrived after decades of development, namely through limited federal support/funding, and increased involvement of employers.

On the federal level, the means-test formulae used to determine who is eligible for subsidized care, or the allowance of tax credits, will likely continue to be manipulated from time-to-time, dependent upon the size of the national debt, state of the economy, value system of the occupants of the White House and Congress, etc. Women's groups, educators, labor unions, and others will likely continue to lobby for liberalization of the distribution of both subsidized care and tax credits, as well as the distribution of vouchers which allow parents to purchase day care at the location of their choice (Marver and Larson, 1978).

On the employer level, we expect increased efforts of organized labor to include child care support, in one form or another, as a fringe benefit in collective bargaining. Federal and state tax-breaks to employers who participate can likely accelerate the process, so lobbying efforts at the national and state levels can ultimately directly affect child care services at the workplace. Such collective bargaining may even include clauses that parents shouldn't lose seniority for taking time off to have a child, and other "parental leave" benefits—such as sick-child care, extended maternity/paternity leaves, and leaves to attend to children during school vacations (Blum, 1983).

In this regard, at the present time, Congress is considering HR-2, legislation that would force businessmen to give workers family leave (a similar bill was vetoed by President Bush in June 1990). The current bill would mandate that businesses give up to 12 weeks of *unpaid* leave to employees at the birth or adoption of children, or when employees or their children, spouses, or parents are seriously ill. Because the law would only apply to companies with 50 or more employees, about 95 percent of all businesses would be exempt, but supporters see it as a start toward federal regulation in this area—especially in industries where organized labor is weak or underrepresented (American Public Health Association, 1991).

At present, day care centers have already been established by some employers, on-site. Sometimes the corporation engages an outside firm to operate the center; sometimes a not-for-profit organization, with a Board consisting of company representatives, operates the center. The corporation often subsidizes the cost of operating the program and provides the service at low cost. Usually the center is located at the workplace and its hours of operation match the parents' work shifts, thus reducing time spent in commuting (Thorman, 1989).

In summary, the expected acceleration in day care services, as we approach the twenty-first century, will be built upon a rethinking of national priorities, in which children come to be viewed as a "national treasure" (Blum, 1983). Governmental involvement will be encouraged, and justified, to the extent that Congress believes that the private sector (already heavily involved) fails to take into account the social needs of *all* children—and not just select groups (Robins and Weiner, 1978). An emphasis on future-oriented programming, while working steadily in the legislative and employment arenas, will likely lead to an expansion of affordable day care for all children, in a society of working parents of both genders (Fein and Clarke-Stewart, 1973).

LIFELONG OCCUPATIONAL COUNSELING

Traditionally, American society has valued the work ethic—related by sociologists to the values of thrift and productivity promoted by the Protestant Ethic which pervaded the country's early social/economic/ political history. In recent years, especially after the so-called "Decade of Greed" of the 1980s, societal forces have been shaping a rethinking of the value and place of work in peoples' lives. Etzioni talks of an alternative society where the main focus is on a host of social values—ranging from concern with the environment, health, culture, and public affairs, to the development of self and meaningful relationships with others. In this scenario, work is not so much avoided as it is placed in a secondary position and judged in its relation to these other priority values (Etzioni, 1979).

Saltzman takes the process a step further by describing the phenomenon of "downshifting"—in which individuals are deliberately placing limits on their careers in order to devote more time to their families, communities, and other needs, in an attempt to lead more "balanced" lives. In the downshifting process, persons are willing to take salary cuts, for example, if they can gain more family and personal time. This disenchantment with the traditional career ladder and "fast-track" may express itself in a number of ways, including (Saltzman, 1991):

• "Back-trackers": who choose self-demotion in order to have more time and less stress.

• "Plateauers": who intentionally stay in place and in control by turning down promotions.

• "Career-shifters": who transfer their skills to less-pressured fields.

• "Self-employers": who go solo for more control over work hours and location of work.

• "Urban escapees": who opt for more hospitable, less-stressful environments.

While the employee actions described above have yet to be studied in large enough numbers to generate a substantial body of research, traditional measures of worker productivity—absenteeism, tardiness, turnover, amount of work, and quality of work have been repeatedly examined for decades (Macarov, 1982). In contrast to such employee-generated action which affects productivity, and the deliberate activities described by Etzioni and Saltzman, are those situations where forced unemployment or underemployment limit workers' productivity against their will. In such instances, some have questioned the State's limited role in unemployment—seeing it as a breach of the social contract between society and the worker. From this perspective, work is seen as part of the fabric of social cohesion and social responsibility, and thus a major concern of the State and its social policies (Marsden, 1975).

Since World War II, there have been major shifts in the American workplace. These have included (Ginzberg, 1974; Freeman, 1979):

- An increase in the number of women in the work force.
- A shift in employment, from blue-collar to white-collar.
- An increase in the number of government employees.
- A substantial increase in the years of schooling required of new entrants into the labor force.
- A shift in jobs away from the Eastern and Midwestern industrial belt, and toward the South, Southwest, and West Coast.

Overlaying these shifts has been the impact of technology on the workplace—an impact that has been massive, powerful, often unpredictable, and sometimes pernicious. As a result, responses to the impact of technology have often been reactive, rather than proactive (Skinner, 1979). Part of the problem is the speed with which much technological change occurs—sometimes resulting in "future shock" when one tries to adapt (Toffler, 1970). As a result of technological impact, the Industrial Revolution of the nineteenth century, which replaced the earlier Agricultural Revolution, is itself being replaced by the High Technology Revolution—also referred to by Toffler as "Super-Industrialism" (Toffler, 1980; Toffler, 1985). The accompanying explosion of knowledge makes it increasingly difficult for professionals to keep abreast of new developments without becoming inundated in their attempts to keep their skills from becoming obsolete (Dubin, 1971, pp. 35–48; Rice, 1990). For those whose skills become obsolete, unemployment, employment at a lower skill-level, or time and money spent in retraining, may be the result (Hall and Miller, 1975; Rakich et al., 1985, p. 405).

Automation, one of the consequences of technological advance, has impacted significantly on production processes which generate goods. Thus, more workers are finding themselves in the service industries where pay, working conditions, and fringe benefits have traditionally been less than satisfactory (Macarov, 1980). Technology is also credited with creating other effects (Macarov, 1991, pp. 93–95):

• The elimination/modification of some dirty, dangerous, disagreeable jobs.

• Removal of interesting aspects of some jobs, resulting in a perception of banality on the part of employees.

• Polarization of work between a few highly-paid, power-wielding, interesting, ego-satisfying jobs, and many low-paying, dull, routine positions.

• Creation of new jobs which tend to be low-paid, requiring low-skill.

• Increased monitoring of workers on the job, regarding time at work, accuracy, speed, etc.—usually by computers—sometimes resulting in increased work-related stress.

• Removal of some of the social satisfaction resulting from informal social networks, by computer technology in particular.

• Increases in the number of contingent workers (part-time, temporary, adjunct), usually with low pay and no fringe benefits.

At the same time that all this has been occurring, workers have been demanding (Walton, 1974):

• Challenges and personal growth on the job, in an age when work is being more simplified and narrowly specialized.

• Egalitarian treatment in the organizational hierarchy.

• Human dignity.

• Immediate gratification.

• Self-esteem and need satisfaction.

The federal government's concern about the employment problem in general, and technological impact in particular, has been expressed in the past decade in several major pieces of legislation. In 1984, the Job Training Partnership Act was passed (Public Law 97-300, July 1, 1984), and related legislation has dealt with such issues as economic dislocation and worker adjustment (U.S. Senate, June 2, 1987; U.S. House of Representatives, 1988), as well as problems of specific groups—such as older workers—those age 55 or more (U.S. General Accounting Office, January, 1990; Hardin and Borus, 1971).

In the meantime, substantive changes in traditional work patterns are occurring. By 1987, 17.3 percent of American workers were defined as part-time (less than 35 hours per week) by the Bureau of the Census (U.S. Department of Commerce, January 1989, Table 629, p. 381), and 12.3 percent of all workers had gone on flexible schedules (U.S. Department of Commerce, January 1989, Table 631, p. 382). Macarov adds that "flexiplace" schedules are also becoming more popular—whereby people are allowed to work at home, usually via computers. This allows workers to care for children or older family members at the same time. Also, job-sharing, where two people hold the same job, getting one salary and dividing the hours of work, is also becoming more popular (Macarov, 1991, pp. 99–100).

Focusing on employers, instead of employees, the National Commission for Employment Policy warns employers that increased domestic and international competition, new technologies, and lagging productivity growth have changed the world of work dramatically. As a result, efficient and effective use of human resources are required. In the next decade, the Commission sees millions of jobs in the goods-producing and service sectors being restructured, to require different—and often new—skills. Large numbers of jobs are expected to be replaced by new occupations, many of which will demand higher-level skills than those eliminated. The Commission, among others, suggests the adoption by American businesses of specific strategies to ensure that their workers have the capabilities needed to adapt to these changes, including (Seitchik et al., July 1990; Toffler, 1990):

- Greater use of incumbents, if appropriate *new* candidates are hard to find.
- Availability of remedial courses on *basic* skills, in addition to retraining and upgrading job-related skills.
- Greater availability to workers of flexitime, flexiplace, child care, and related conveniences.

One may well ask, what role is the human services worker to play in the fast-changing world of work? Traditionally, social workers have been concerned with getting people off welfare rolls and into jobs. Approaches have included (Huttman, 1981, p. 186):

- Introducing job training programs in cooperation with the Department of Labor and having recipients simultaneously receive training *and* welfare.
- Giving people incentives to work while on welfare.
- Providing public employment jobs and encouraging private industry to provide apprentice or trainee positions through tax incentives or payments to each trainee.
- Making it mandatory that those considered employable report to the employment office and accept jobs or training.

• Providing day care for welfare mothers going into training or employment.

An overriding concern regarding welfare recipients has been the provision of incentives for poor people to work in the face of unearned income. For centuries, fear has been expressed that welfare recipients will refuse to work if they can get the same, or less than they can receive, when not working—or that they will refuse to work under any circumstances (Macarov, 1970). As a result, social workers have spent considerable effort to help clients find work, motivate them, and prepare them to perform and hold their jobs. Work is a measuring rod for individuals, a goal of organizations, and a basis of society. As such, it is seen as both necessary and desirable, and political, social, and economic programs are built on the assumption that people want and need to work, and that society needs all the work that laborers are capable of producing. To not work—by choice or accident—is to be viewed outside the mainstream (Macarov, 1991).

The forces currently affecting the economy in general, and the workplace in particular, and expected to accelerate in impact in the coming decade, will spare few—if any—in the workplace. While everyone's job will not be in comparable jeopardy due to foreign competition, technological advances, etc., to some degree, all will likely need to consider career adjustments, retraining (or at the least, continuing education), and assistance in coping with forces which may be beyond individual control. To assist in this task, the HSW described in Part III of this volume, can make relevant contributions. The functions of assessment, referral, client advocacy, coordination, and evaluation put the HSW in the position to assist in, and offer, the kind of "lifelong occupational counseling" the future is likely to demand. The notion that one will choose a career at an early age, train for it, work for 40 years with no additional/updated skills, and for the same employer until retirement, is less and less likely to be the case. The HSW is capable of bringing a holistic, systems approach to the lifelong need many of us will have for occupational counseling. At the present time, we see two main models for the HSW in this arena, which we will call the traditional and the futuristic.

In the traditional model, HSWs will assist individuals with referral to community programs/agencies where entry-level skills may be obtained. Also, referral will be made for those who are already skilled but need updating/retraining. In the role of coordinator, the HSW will be doing on the local level what the federal government attempted by the Education and Training Partnership Act—to obtain better coordination between training and employment programs (U.S. Senate, February 19 and 25, 1986). Of particular concern will be hard-to-place adults and youth who need continuing attention, for some time, before they are relatively stabilized in the marketplace. The Job Training Partnership Act provides federal grants to the states which can be used in these cooperative efforts (U.S. Senate, July 1, and 2 and August 7, 1985; U.S. House of Representatives, September 24, 1990). The philosophy in the traditional model of lifelong occupational counseling is that most, if not all, workers will need the skills of a professionally-trained HSW at one or more points in their working years, and such an individual is in an excellent position to motivate, refer for training, advocate, coordinate, and evaluate this lifelong need to earn a living, and how well it is being met.

In the futuristic model, the picture is more bleak and departs radically from tradition. Here, the unemployment problem is aggravated by continued reduction in work hours, continued growth of aged populations in general—and the aging "baby boom" generation in particular, and continued growth of structural unemployment (Macarov, 1980). In this model, additional education may be of limited value, if the jobs simply *don't* exist. Even professionals, in such an instance, may find themselves obsolete—to the extent of having to cope with demotions or early retirement (Belbin, 1971). At the same time, desires for lifelong job-security will be frustrated in such a marketplace (Seitchik et al., July 1990). Macarov sees the future problems of unemployment as including (Macarov, 1991):

• Greater urgency than even at present.

• Decreased need for human labor due to future technological developments.

• Greater reductions in the number of full-time jobs available.

• The creation of a class of "permanently unemployed"—who have little in the way of skills, market knowledge, positive work habits and contacts in the marketplace.

Macarov suggests that so many will be unemployed, or underemployed, in this scenario, that a new perspective will be required of the HSW, departing from the prior focus on helping the client find or keep a job—as described in the traditional model (above). In his view, the client should be helped to find a fulfilling life *despite* the lack of a traditional job. He/she should be counseled by the HSW, or those to whom the HSW makes referral, not to feel stigmatized by this situation, and to maintain a positive self-image despite it all. Of course, for this perspective to be practical, a radical change in social values and attitudes toward labor must occur—allowing other attributes and activities, besides traditional work, to become valued and important. Resources, for instance, will have to be distributed on some basis other than job-related work done. Macarov suggests payment for "informal work"—housekeeping, care of children, care of elderly relatives. If such activities are recognized by society as being of value, the alternate sources of respect, friendship, and status will emerge (Macarov, 1991). In the event that this futuristic model emerges, we believe the HSW, as described herein, can assist the permanently formally unemployed Macarov discusses, to lead more satisfying lives, in a complex economic environment.

The problems of unemployment and underemployment are no longer seen as individual, low-profile problems. Whether the coming decade will see these problems on a par with American experience during the Great Depression, remains to be seen. Certainly, modern communication media bring the problem home—whether local or national—every day in newspaper and television reports. Governmental bodies, educational institutions, voluntary agencies, and private industry have applied a variety of solutions to at least selective parts of the problem. Agencies such as the U.S. Department of Commerce, Social Security Administration, Bureau of the Census, labor unions, academic researchers, and others, have generated data on the complexities of the world of work in this day and age. Lobbying efforts have motivated both the federal government and the respective states to deal with specific pieces of the problem. And while one may argue that additional federal involvement is needed to establish clear, workable national policies and objectives on the issue of employment (Zagoria, 1974), we believe there is a role for the HSW to play in assisting persons in need of lifelong occupational counseling.

AID-IN-DYING SERVICES FOR THE TERMINALLY ILL

As indicated elsewhere in this book, important changes have occurred since the turn of the century which have impacted significantly upon the human services. One of these has been the increase in longevity, resulting in a significant population of elderly (those over 65 years of age). According to the American Association of Retired Persons, 12.4 percent of the U.S. population was over age 65 in 1988. Projections for the year 2000 are 13 percent, and for the year 2030, due to the aging of the post-World War

II "baby boom generation," the figure is expected to rise to 21.8 percent (American Association of Retired Persons, 1989). In Florida, which has the largest proportion of residents in this age range, the comparable figure in 1987 was 18.1 percent (Bureau of Economic and Business Research, 1988).

Scientific advances over many common communicable diseases have contributed to this situation, with the result that chronic disease among the elderly is now a major concern. Technological advances have made it possible to *treat* many chronic diseases indefinitely, even if they cannot be *cured.* One result is continued pain and suffering, over a long period of time, for some persons (Weissburg and Hartz, 1983; Mishkin, 1985; Cohen, 1988). Another is catastropic health care costs, in a time of rapid inflation in the medical marketplace. Thus, financial pressure is often added to the burden of illness itself, creating profound emotional distress.

As this situation has escalated, values have begun to shift in American society. People are coming to question, more and more, the value of extending the *quantity* of life at the expense of the *quality* of life (Lamm, 1990). As a result, discussions of euthanasia have become more prominent than ever.

Euthanasia may be defined as the act or practice (for reasons of mercy) of terminating the lives of individuals (active euthanasia) or allowing them to die without giving all possible treatments for their diseases (passive euthanasia) because they are hopelessly sick or injured (Goldstein, 1989, p. 90; U.S. House of Representatives, 1976, p. 55). In a recent scientifically-designed survey, 64 percent of respondents indicated that physicians should not be charged/prosecuted if they help the fatally ill commit suicide, and 80 percent indicated they would want life support systems disconnected if they were in a coma from which physicians believed they would not recover (Reuters News Service, May 6, 1991).

The issue of euthanasia is a very old one. In pre-Christian times, suicide was seen as sometimes the wisest course of action, and as such, not necessarily an irrational or dishonorable act—particularly when practiced by those in advanced age. The evolving concept of "rational preemptive suicide" usually contains such prerequisites as ability to reason, having a realistic world view, having adequate information upon which to make decisions, avoidance of harm to others, and action consistent with one's fundamental interests (Prado, 1990). The previous popularity of the practice in ancient Greece and Rome officially came to an end from at least the 5th Century, and definitely with the arrival of the Justinian Code of the 6th Century (Riga, 1981).

The issue of euthanasia is also a complex one, and perhaps the best single source for an introductory reading on *all* sides of the issue is Greenhaven Press' "opposing viewpoints" volume on the subject. This comprehensive book deals with such issues as ethics, policies, criteria, decision-making processes, etc. The material presented in the book is taken from a wide variety of sources. In general, the euthanasia proponents represented here emphasize the physical/social/economic consequences of prolonged suffering and dying, the futility of "aggressive life-saving measures" in some instances, the de facto occurrence of euthanasia—even without current legal sanction, and the issue of quality of life versus quantity of life. Euthanasia opponents emphasize the "playing God dilemma" for those who make euthanasia decisions, the fear of a "slippery slope effect"—leading to the wholesale class exterminations practiced in Nazi Germany, the historical antieuthanasia stance of Western societies, the problem of conflict of interest when family members are allowed to make such decisions for the patient, etc. (Bernards, 1989).

The issue is one of great complexity, requiring an interdisciplinary approach. As a result, when the Hastings Center established a research group in 1985 to focus on questions regarding the treatment and care of the dying, they included physicians, nurses, philosophers, lawyers, and health care administrators. The resulting guidelines they established are to assist health care professionals, patients, surrogates responsible for making decisions about the use of life-sustaining treatment, policy makers, scholars, and others (Hastings Center, 1987).

On the legal front, there is a common law tradition in America that one who assists another in committing suicide, either by furnishing the means, or by assisting in any way, is guilty of murder. Some jurisdictions, preferring not to rely solely on common law tradition, have enacted statutes making it a crime to aid, advise, or encourage another to commit suicide. Every modern legal system considers euthanasia a crime, but few punish it as severely as the Anglo-American system. This common law tradition was influenced by Christian philosophy, which regarded life as sacred and inalienable, and is reflected in criminal law as well. This is an absolutist view which tends to consider humanitarian motives for killing as irrelevant, no matter how hopeless or pitiable the situation. The motive of the accused is not considered a defense for euthanasia, in theory. In actuality, judges and juries have *obviously* considered motive in some cases of euthanasia (Riga, 1981).

At the heart of the legal issue is the question of whether one has a right to die, based on the "free exercise clause" of the First Amendment of the U.S. Constitution. On a number of issues in the past (polygamy, conscientious objection to war, etc.), free exercise has often lost, in favor of the argument that there is a compelling, overriding *state* interest. Thus, the free exercise issue is ambiguous. A more decisive argument is that based on a constitutional "right to privacy" for voluntary euthanasia, where one could argue that a terminally-ill patient has a right to die quickly and peacefully, in private (Riga, 1981). A third argument, the "quality of life" argument, has become part and parcel of the hospice philosophy discussed earlier (Cohen, 1979). While the hospice movement has been very careful to stress that it is *not* advocating euthanasia—and has spent considerable effort in so doing, especially when attempting to gain community acceptance—it stresses not only the right of terminally-ill patients to freely make private decisions regarding their dying, but also the legitimacy of balancing concerns over quantity of life with life's quality (Harrison and Richie, 1988).

In 1938, the Euthanasia Society of America was founded, to attempt to legalize the right to a "good death." Later, the organization changed its name to the Society for the Right to Die, and most recently became Concern for Dying. The organization originated the "living will" (discussed below), and functions as a not-for-profit educational organization which relies on financial contributions. A corollary movement, the Hemlock Society, was founded by Derek Humphry, after he assisted his cancer-stricken first wife, Jean, in her suicide (National Hemlock Society, 1988; Humphry, 1983; Humphry and Wickett, 1986; Humphry and Wickett, 1990; Humphry, 1991; Blake, 1983).

In 1976, California became the first state to enact a Natural Death or Living Will Act. Since then, 40 other states have also done so, as of 1990 (Pozgar, 1990, p. 195). The National Conference of Commissioners for Uniform State Laws has attempted for years to shepherd comparable right-to-die bills throughout the United States, to make the right available to all, despite residence (National Conference of Commissioners on Uniform State Laws, 1985). At the same time, it should be pointed out that there have been opponents to the legalization of living wills, such as the National Doctors for Life, headquartered in St. Louis, Missouri (U.S. House of Representatives, October 1, 1985, pp. 90–91).

Concern for Dying distributes sample forms of living wills, as well as forms for durable power of attorney for health care decision-makers (Society for the Right to Die, 1985; Concern for Dying, 1990). As an indication of the value to physicians of the lawful, correct and timely completion of such forms by patients, the Florida Medical Association currently distributes such documents, as well as information on current right-to-die legislation in the state—legislation which allows the terminally-ill patient to not only indicate he/she does not want life-prolonging procedures employed, but that he/she also wants withdrawal/withholding of artificially-administered nutrition/hydration (Florida Medical Association, 1990; Florida Statute 745.41–.52, 1990; Florida Statute 765.01–.15, 1990).

The right-to-die has now been recognized by most courts and accepted by a majority in our society as a basic human right (Riga, 1981). However, the process was a difficult one. Before its legitimization, some likely died unnecessarily-prolonged deaths, while others were surreptitiously treated by sympathetic physicians who either withheld life-prolonging treatment before the enactment of living will legislation in their states, or may even have accelerated the dying process by gradually increasing the dosage of drugs capable of ending life, as well as reducing pain.

By the mid-1980s, these, and related, issues were of significant national concern to provoke a presidential commission to examine the ethical aspects of foregoing life-sustaining treatment (President's Commission for the Study of Ethical Problems in Medicine and Biomedical and Behavioral Research, March 1983). Congress also became involved in the dying-with-dignity debate as well (U.S. House of Representatives, October 1, 1985). While legal debates were in progress, and scholarly groups considered the issues of right-to-die, in reality health care providers and patients were making daily decisions, usually in a low-profile manner. Orders against resuscitation were common in hospitals, whereby the ability to rescue a patient from the brink of death by restoring life-giving heartbeat and breathing was deliberately not employed through "no code" (do not resuscitate) orders (Rabkin et al., 1976). Thanks to technology, even the definition of "death" became problematic, and added ambiguity to the dying process and clarity of medical decision-making (President's Commission for the Study of Ethical Problems in Medicine and Biomedical and Behavioral Research, July 1981).

Much of the drama over the right-to-die has been played out in the courtroom over the past several decades. Perhaps the most widely-publicized case was that of Karen Ann Quinlan, where the New Jersey

Supreme Court eventually declared that a patient has the right to decline medical treatment under certain circumstances as part of the constitutional right of privacy (In re Quinlan, 1976). In Florida, important cases have been those that declared competent persons have a constitutional right to refuse medical treatment (Satz v. Perlmutter, 1980) and that incompetent patients may have medical treatment refused *on their behalf* by an authorized representative (John F. Kennedy Memorial Hospital, Inc. v. The Hon. David H. Bludworth, 1984). The right to withdraw life-prolonging procedures *after* they have been initiated has also been recognized in Florida (Corbett v. D'Alessandro, 1986).

The State of Washington is currently considering a bill that will go far beyond the issue of right-to-die, living wills, durable power of attorney for health care decisions, etc. Initiative 119 (also called the Death with Dignity Act) will allow voters to decide by referendum in November 1991 if they want a law allowing terminally-ill persons with less than six months to live to be able to ask a physician to help them die by lethal injection or some other means. Viewed as "aid-in-dying" (a euphemism for active euthanasia), this procedure is seen as a medical service, to be provided only by a physician, to a conscious, mentally-competent, adult patient, who meets the medical criteria for terminal illness (attested by two physicians). The directive is to be voluntary, written, part of the patient's clinical record, and revokable at any time. The Washington State initiative will recognize similar directives lawfully executed in other states. An important part of the proposal is that it protects persons who act in good faith in accord with the law, from criminal, civil, or administrative liability. It also allows physicians and health care facilities to refuse to participate, but in such instances, they are obligated to make a good faith effort to transfer the patient to another physician and/or facility. Because of the frequent invalidation of life insurance policies in the case of suicide, the proposal forbids such invalidation, or negative effects of any kind, on the sale, issuance, or pay-out of such policies. It also allows for prosecution, on charges of murder in the first degree, of any person who falsifies, forces the directive of another, or willfully conceals/withholds personal knowledge of a revocation by the patient—which leads to the service being provided (State of Washington, January 18, 1991).

While the fate of the Washington State initiative is being decided, and while legislators in other states may be considering aid-in-dying legislation, we have the example of actual practice in the Netherlands—a European country with a high standard of living. As in the other countries of western Europe, active euthanasia is technically a crime in the Netherlands also. And as in many other countries, including the United States, it is possible to find courts and juries which have been lenient when considering the defendant's motives—especially when there has appeared to be a "conflict of duties" or an emergency situation requiring quick action (Gevers, 1987).

Contrary to popular belief, the government of the Netherlands has not adopted a law legalizing euthanasia. Instead, it has decided that physicians who terminate life on request of a patient will *not* be punished if they: (1) invoke a defense of "force majeure," i.e. they were subjected to irresistible or superior forces which were difficult to foresee/control (Ballentine, 1969, p. 1347; Black, 1990, p. 645); (2) have satisfied certain criteria (to be discussed below); and (3) the court accepts the defense in these particular circumstances. Thus, the physician practicing aid-in-dying in the Netherlands is technically in violation of the law. In practice, however, he/she will not likely be prosecuted if the following strict guidelines—affirmed by the Royal Dutch Medical Association and the State Commission on Euthanasia in 1985—have been met, and the court accepts the force majeure defense (Rigter, 1989; de Roy van Zuydewijn, 1987):

• the patient's request must be explicit/repeated, leaving no reason for doubt concerning the desire to die.

• the mental and/or physical suffering of the patient must be very severe, without prospect of relief.

• the patient's decision must be an informed one, voluntarily made.

• all options for other care must have been exhausted or refused by the patient.

• the attending physician must have consulted with another physician (he/she may *also* consult with nurses, the clergy, and others, as well).

• a detailed record must be kept of the course of events.

It is expected that those physicians who adhere to these guidelines will face minimal judicial "red tape," although they are not exempt from prosecution. A study of aid-in-dying cases in Amsterdam in 1987 indicated that of almost 300 cases, only 10 percent were reported to the public prosecutor, placing the physicians involved in the position of possibly having to plead force majeure and document satisfaction of the above guidelines—if the prosecutor chose to act on the report. Another Dutch study estimates that the average general practitioner in the Netherlands will have recourse to euthanasia about once every three years. It is believed there is no economic incentive for Dutch physicians to expedite aid-in-dying, as they actually lose income when a patient succumbs, since they are paid on a per capita basis under the state health care system (Rigter, 1989).

As far as the Dutch populace is concerned, a survey regarded as reliable and valid found 68 percent of the population as a whole, and 69 percent of Roman Catholics—despite condemnation of aid-in-dying by the Dutch Bishops—to be in favor of *full* legalization, in accord with the criteria stated above. In general, the Dutch believe their approach, while not fully legal, brings the issue more out into the open than in most other countries, and at the same time makes the physician understand that he/she must *always* be prepared to answer to the law (de Roy van Zuydewijn, 1987; Gevers, 1987).

However the Washington State initiative is decided, and whatever occurs in other countries, a host of forces are crystallizing at the end of the twentieth century to suggest that aid-in-dying legislation in the United States is not far off. Like the right-to-die legislation, the process will probably start in a single state (perhaps Washington) and once a law is enacted, and upheld in the courts, pressure will build for similar legal rights for all Americans, regardless of residence. The once secretive, tragic, painful process of dying for many terminally-ill people has now been brought out into the open by patients themselves, their surrogates, legislators, the courts, and others. Media attention is intense because of the exacerbation of technology, economic factors, medical advances, and aging. Solutions once considered radical, even forbidden, are being tried, and data are accumulating, indicating the prevalence of the problem, and the wishes of the public. Through continued lobbying, concerned citizens are expected to attempt to influence their legislators in this matter during the coming decade.

SUMMARY ON FORTHCOMING HUMAN SERVICES

In varying degree, the five human services described in this part of the book have arrived at different stages of development as the 20th Century hastens toward its close. While all five are not at the same level of advancement, we believe all will attain significant development over the coming decade. Table 3 summarizes the relationship between each of these five services and the evolutionary model presented in Figure 2.

Table 3. The Evolutionary Progress of Selected Human Services.

Evolutionary Stage	Human Service				
	National Health Insurance	Services for the Homeless	Day Care for Children	Lifelong Occupational Counseling	Aid-in-dying Services for the Terminally Ill
Stage 1:					
The issue is perceived as an individual problem, and has a low-profile status to overcome.	Health care costs are now a universal concern — everyone fears them.	A significant increase in the homelessness of the previously employed has occurred.	A significant increase in the number of working women has occurred.	Unemployment/underemployment have reached into the working class to a significant degree.	The hospice movement and other forces have given the dying process heightened visibility.
Stage 2:					
The problem receives considerable attention in the media.	Daily media reports are presented on the high cost of health care.	Much media attention has been given to the entrance of families and the formerly regularly employed into the ranks of the homeless.	Working mothers and feminist groups have become more vocal and organized, attracting media attention.	The media have given increasing attention to the problem, which is now seen as national, and not just regional.	The media have exploited the more sensationalistic aspects of this issue.
Stage 3:					
Pioneering solutions are offered/attempted.	Local, state and Federal, as well as voluntary and private solutions, have been attempted.	Voluntary and governmental solutions have been attempted.	Private, voluntary and governmental solutions have been attempted.	Voluntary and governmental solutions, with some assistance from private industry, have been attempted.	The voluntary sector has predominated, with recent movement by the government — through legislation and court decisions.

Table 3. The Evolutionary Progress of Selected Human Services.

Evolutionary Stage	Human Service				
	National Health Insurance	*Services for the Homeless*	*Day Care for Children*	*Lifelong Occupational Counseling*	*Aid-in-dying Services for the Terminally Ill*
Stage 4: Statistical data and research findings are made available.	A wealth of data are available on all aspects of health care financing.	Data have been gathered on the number of homeless, the types of homeless, and the causes of homelessness.	Data on the number of children of working mothers, in and out of day care, are available, as well as data on the services available.	Data on the number of unemployed and the reasons, are routinely collected— and estimates of underemployment are also now being made.	Data on the terminally ill, the number of hospice patients, number completing living wills, and related statistics, are available.
Stage 5: The government becomes highly involved in the problem, through administrative action or legislation.	The next logical step in the progression of governmental involvement would be some form of national health insurance.	The entrance of working families into the ranks of the homeless will likely spur governmental solutions—if not nationally, then locally.	As the composition of families continues to change, along with values, the government will be asked to provide incentives to employers to assist in this matter.	Because of the importance of work in our society and the need for a productive citizenry, greater involvement of the government, directly or indirectly, is expected.	A progression of legislation has increasingly given priority to the individual's right to make important final decisions, and is expected to continue.

CONCLUSION OF THE BOOK

In this volume, we have attempted firstly to examine the evolution of human services in the United States, particularly over the past century. We have seen that a combination of governmental, voluntary and private efforts have been made—with varying degrees of success and enthusiasm.

In the final decade of this century, a host of common human needs have precipitated a demand for new human services, such as hospices for the terminally ill and AIDS services agencies. An evolutionary model evolved, which illustrates the process by which many individual problems progress to a community-action level, and later to the national arena.

In order to cope with the complexity of human service problems, and provide a coordinated, systems approach, we proposed the establishment of the professional occupational category of Human Services Worker (HSW), with a distinct role, specific functions, and professional education/training.

In view of the continuing evolution of human needs, as well as the services to meet them, we ended this volume with a discussion of several human services we expect will undergo substantial development as the twenty-first century dawns. It is our hope that society will increasingly become responsive to its citizens, and to meeting their legitimate need for human services—be they provided by government, voluntary agencies, or the private sector.

REFERENCES

Ainslie, Ricardo C., (ed.). *The Child and the Day Care Setting.* New York: Praeger, 1984.

Albritton, Phyllis M. "Access to Health Care: A U.S. Congressional Staffer's Perspective on a National Problem." *Henry Ford Hospital Medical Journal,* Vol. 38, Nos. 2 & 3, 1990, pp. 108–109.

Alpha Center. *Health Care for the Uninsured Program Update.* Washington, DC: 1350 Connecticut Avenue, NW, No. 11, April 1991.

American Association of Retired Persons. *A Profile of Older Americans—1989.* Washington, DC: AARP, 1989.

American Public Health Association. "Family Leave Bill Moving," *The Nation's Health,* April 1991, p. 7.

Anderson, Odin. *Blue Cross Since 1929: Accountability and the Public Trust.* Cambridge, MA: Ballinger, 1975.

Applebaum, Richard P. "Counting the Homeless," in *Homelessness in the United States,* Jamshid A. Momeni, (ed.)., New York: Praeger, 1990, Chapter 1, pp. 1–16.

Auerbach, Stevanne. *The Child Care Crisis.* Boston: Beacon Press, 1979.

Babcock, C. Patrick. "Health Care: A Universal Right." *Henry Ford Hospital Medical Journal,* Vol. 38, Nos. 2 & 3, 1990, pp. 101–102.

Bachman, George and Lewis Meriam. *The Issue of Compulsory Health Insurance.* New York: ARNO Press, 1976.

Ballentine, James. *Ballentine's Law Dictionary — 3rd Edition.* San Francisco: Bancroft-Whitney, 1969.

Balog, James. "Are We Climbing the Wall of Resistance Toward National Health Insurance?," in *A Call for Action: Final Report,* Pepper Commission — U.S. Bipartisan Commission on Comprehensive Health Care. Washington, DC: Government Printing Office, September 1990, pp. 148–153.

Beck, Rochelle. "Beyond Stalemate in Child Care Public Policy," in *Day Care: Scientific and Social Policy Issues,* by E.F. Zigler and E.W. Gordon, (eds.)., Boston: Auburn House, 1982, Chapter 16, pp. 307–337.

Belbin, R.M. "Mid-Career Education: Its Shape as a Function of Human Disequilibrium," in *Professional Obsolescence,* Samuel Dubin, (ed.)., Lexington, MA: Lexington Books, 1971, pp. 72–78.

Benfer, David and Vinod Sahney. "Sounding the Alarm: A Need for Health Care Reform." *Henry Ford Hospital Medical Journal,* Vol. 38, Nos. 2 & 3, 1990, p. 100.

Berki, S.E. "Approaches to Financing Care for the Uninsured." *Henry Ford Hospital Medical Journal,* Vol. 38, Nos. 2 & 3, 1990, pp. 119–122.

Berkowitz, Edward D. "Wilbur Cohen and American Social Reform," *Social Work,* Vol. 34, No. 4, July 1989, pp. 293–299.

Bernards, Neil, (ed.). *Euthanasia: Opposing Viewpoints.* San Diego: Greenhaven Press, 1989.

Black, Henry Campbell. *Black's Law Dictionary — 6th Edition.* St. Paul: West, 1990.

Blake, Patricia. "Going Gentle into that Good night," *Time,* March 21, 1983, p. 85.

Blum, Marion. *The Day Care Dilemma.* Lexington, MA: Lexington Books, 1983.

Bowen, Elizabeth L. "Health, Safety and Nutritional Requirements of Young Children," in *Administering Day Care and Preschool Programs,* by Donald Streets, (ed.)., Boston: Allyn and Bacon, 1982, Chapter VI, pp. 128–161.

Brickner, Philip, (ed.). *Under the Safety Net: The Health and Social Welfare of the Homeless in the United States.* New York: W.W. Norton, 1990.

Bureau of Economic and Business Research. *1988 Florida Statistical Abstract.* Gainesville, FL: The University Presses of Florida, 1988.

Burt, Martha R. and Barbara E. Cohen. "A Sociodemographic Profile of the Service-Using Homeless: Findings from a National Survey," in *Homelessness in the United States,* Jamshid A. Momeni, (ed.)., New York: Praeger, 1990, Chapter 2, pp. 17–38.

Buss, Terry. "Public Policies for Reducing Homelessness in America," in *Homelessness in the United States,* Jamshid A. Momeni, (ed.)., New York: Praeger, 1990, Chapter 10, pp. 153–164.

Camp, Sharon and J. Joseph Speidel. *The International Human Suffering Index.* Washington, DC: Population Crisis Committee, 1987.

Child Welfare League of America. *Standards for Day Care Service.* New York: CWLA, 1969.

Clarke-Stewart, A. *Daycare.* Cambridge: Harvard University Press, 1982.

Cohen, Cynthia B., (ed.). *Casebook on the Termination of Life-Sustaining Treatment and the Care of the Dying.* Bloomington: Indiana University Press, 1988.

Cohen, Kenneth. *Hospice — Prescription for Terminal Care.* Germantown, MD: Aspen Systems, 1979.

Concern for Dying. *Living Wills.* New York: Concern for Dying, 250 W. 57th Street, New York 10107, 1990.

Corbett v. D'Alessandro, 487 So. 2d. 368 (Fla. Dist. Ct. App. 1986).

Corpus, Larry D. and Kathleen M. Corpus. "Mass Flea Outbreak at a Child Care Facility: Case Report," *American Journal of Public Health,* Vol. 81, No. 4, April 1991, pp. 497–498.

Daly, Gerald. "Programs Dealing with Homelessness in the United States, Canada and Britain," in *Homelessness in the United States,* Jamshid A. Momeni, (ed.)., New York, Praeger, 1990, Chapter 9, pp. 133–152.

Davis, Karen and Diane Rowland. "Uninsured and Underinsured: Inequalities in Health Care in the United States," in *The Nation's Health,* Philip R. Lee and Carroll L. Estes, (eds.)., Boston: Jones and Bartlett, 1990, Chapter 7, pp. 298–308.

DeMiguel, Jesus. "A Framework for the Study of National Health Systems," *Inquiry — Supplement to Vol. XII,* No. 2:13, June 1975, pp. 10–24.

Department of Health and Rehabilitative Services. *Homeless Conditions in Florida.* Tallahassee, FL: DHRS, June 30, 1990.

Dluhy, Milan J. "How to Help Dade County's Homeless," Miami: *Miami Herald,* January 13, 1991, pp. 1C and 6C.

Dubin, Samuel. "Motivating Factors in Professional Updating," in *Professional Obsolescence,* Samuel Dubin, (ed.)., Lexington, MA: Lexington Books, 1971, pp. 35–48.

de Roy van Zuydewijn, H.J. *Euthanasia in the Netherlands.* The Hague: Health Council of the Netherlands, March 23, 1987.

Eilers, Robert and Sue Moyerman. *National Health Insurance: Proceedings of the Conference on National Health Insurance.* Homewood, IL: Richard D. Irwin, 1971.

Elling, Ray H. *Cross-National Study of Health Systems.* New Brunswick, NJ: Transaction Books, 1980.

Etzioni, Amitai. "Work in the American Future: Reindustrialization or Quality of Life?," in *Work in America: The Decade Ahead,* Clark Kerr and Jerome Rosow, (eds.)., New York: Van Nostrand Reinhold, 1979, Chapter 2, pp. 27–34.

Federation of American Health Systems Review. "The National Health Policy Debate," *FAHS Review,* May/June 1990, pp. 17–22.

Fein, Greta G. and Alison Clarke-Stewart. *Day Care in Context.* New York: John Wiley and Sons, 1973.

Fike, David. *The South Florida Homeless Studies — Proposal.* Miami, FL: Barry University, 1988.

Florida Medical Association. *Your Health Care Surrogate: For Peace of Mind.* Jacksonville, FL: Florida Medical Association, 1990.

Florida Statute 745.41–.52: Health Care Surrogate Act, 1990.

Florida Statute 765.01–.15: Right to Decline Life-Prolonging Procedures Act, October 1, 1990.

Freeman, Richard B. "The Work Force of the Future: An Overview," in *Work in*

America: The Decade Ahead, Clark Kerr and Jerome Rosow, (eds.)., New York: Van Nostrand Reinhold, 1979, Chapter 4, pp. 58–79.

Gevers, J.K.M. "Legal Developments Concerning Active Euthanasia on Request in the Netherlands," *Bioethics,* Vol. 1, No. 2, 1987, pp. 156–162.

Ginzberg, Eli. "The Changing American Economy and Labor Force," in *The Worker and the Job: Coping with Change,* Jerome M. Rosow, (ed.)., Englewood Cliffs, NJ: Prentice-Hall, 1974, Chapter 2, pp. 49–71.

Goldstein, Arnold. *Dictionary of Health Care Administration.* Rockville, MD: Aspen, 1989.

Habitat for Humanity International, Inc. *Habitat World,* Vol. 8, No. 1, February 1991.

Hagen, Jan L. and Elizabeth Hutchison. "Who's Serving the Homeless?" *Social Casework: The Journal of Contemporary Social Work,* October 1988, pp. 491–497.

Hall, Kenneth and Isobel Miller. *Retraining and Tradition: The Skilled Worker in an Era of Change.* London: George Allen and Unwin, Ltd., 1975.

Hardin, Einar and Michael E. Borus. *The Economic Benefits and Costs of Retraining.* Lexington, MA: Lexington Books, 1971.

Harrison, Mary and Nicholas D. Richie. "The First Decade: A Hospice Case Study," *The American Journal of Hospice Care,* Vol. 5, No. 6, November/December 1988, pp. 43–47.

Hastings Center. *Guidelines on the Termination of Life-Sustaining Treatment and the Care of the Dying.* Briarcliff Manor, NY: The Hastings Center, 1987.

Hatch, Orrin G. "Families, Children and Child Care," in *Day Care: Scientific and Social Policy Issues,* E.F. Zigler and E.W. Gordon, (eds.)., Boston: Auburn House, 1982, Chapter 13, pp. 255–259.

Health Insurance Association of America. *Source Book of Health Insurance Data — 1990.* Washington, DC: HIAA, 1990.

Heller, Wendy M. et al. "Ethnic and Cultural Diversity in Day Care Programming," in *Administering Day Care and Preschool Programs,* Donald Streets, (ed.)., Boston: Allyn and Bacon, 1982, Chapter IV, pp. 88–109.

Hopps, June Gary. "Presidential Priorities and a Social Work Agenda," *Social Work,* Vol. 43, No. 2, March 1989, pp. 99–100.

Humphry, Derek. *Let Me Die Before I Wake.* New York: Grove-Weidenfeld, 1983.

Humphry, Derek and Ann Wickett. *Jean's Way.* New York: Harper and Row, 1986.

Humphry, Derek and Ann Wickett. *The Right to Die: Understanding Euthanasia.* Eugene, OR: The Hemlock Society, 1990.

Humphry, Derek. *Final Exit: Self-Deliverance and Assisted Suicide for the Dying.* Eugene, OR: The Hemlock Society, 1991.

Huttman, Elizabeth. *Introduction to Social Policy.* New York: McGraw-Hill, 1981.

In re Quinlan, 70 N.J. 10, 355 A. 2d 647, 662–63, cert. denied, 429 U.S. 922 (1976).

John F. Kennedy Memorial Hospital v. The Hon. David H. Bludworth, 452 So. 2d 921 (Florida, 1984).

Kahn, A. and S. Kamerman. *Child Care: Facing the Hard Choices.* Dover, MA: Auburn House 1987.

Karger, Howard J. and David Stoesz. *American Social Welfare Policy: A Structural Approach.* New York: Longman, 1990.

Katz, Lillian Gorshaw. "Ethical Issues in Working with Young Children," in *Administering Day Care and Preschool Programs,* Donald Streets, (ed.). Boston: Allyn and Bacon, 1982, Chapter V, pp. 112–125.

Kennedy, Edward M. "Child Care—A Commitment to be Honored", in *Day Care: Scientific and Social Policy Issues,* E.F. Zigler and E.W. Gordon, (eds.). Boston: Auburn House 1982, Chapter 14, pp. 260–263.

Lamm, Richard D. "The Ten Commandments of Health Care," in *The Nation's Health,* Philip R. Lee and Carroll L. Estes, (eds.). Boston: Jones and Bartlett, 1990, Chapter 3, pp. 124–133.

Macarov, David. *Incentives to Work.* San Francisco: Jossey-Bass, 1970.

Macarov, David. *Work and Welfare: The Unholy Alliance.* Beverly Hills: Sage, 1980.

Macarov, David. *Worker Productivity: Myths and Reality.* Beverly Hills: Sage, 1982.

Macarov, David. *Certain Change: Social Work Practice in the Future.* Silver Spring, MD: National Association of Social Workers, 1991.

Marsden, Dennis. *Workless: Some Unemployed Men and their Families.* Baltimore: Penguin Books, 1975.

Martin, George T. *Social Policy in the Welfare State.* Englewood Cliffs, NJ: Prentice-Hall, 1990.

Marver, James D. and Meredith A. Larson. "Public Policy Toward Child Care in America: A Historical Perspective," in *Child Care and Public Policy,* by Philip K. Robins and Samuel Weiner, (eds.)., Lexington, MA: Lexington Books, 1978, Chapter 2, pp. 17–42.

Maynard, Fredelle. *The Child Care Crisis.* New York: Viking Press, 1985.

McGarrahan, Ellen. "Bill to Regulate In-Home Day Care." Miami, FL: *The Miami Herald,* April 24, 1991, p. 14A.

Mishkin, Barbara. "Decisions Concerning the Terminally Ill: How to Protect Patients, Staff and the Hospital," *Health Span — The Report of Health, Business and Law,* Vol. 2, No. 3, March 1985, pp. 17–21.

Momeni, Jamshid A. *Homelessness in the United States.* New York, Praeger, 1990.

Monheit, A. and C. Schur. *Health Insurance Coverage of Retired Persons.* DHHS Pub. No. (PHS) 89-3444, Rockville, MD: NCHSR&HCTA, September 1989.

Moss, M. Scott. "National Health Care Proposed by NASW Would Save U.S. Billions, Analysts Find." *NASW News.* Silver Spring, MD: National Association of Social Workers, Vol. 36, No. 2, February 1991, pp. 1 and 14.

National Conference of Commissioners on Uniform State Laws. *Uniform Rights of the Terminally Ill Act.* Minneapolis: Commission on Uniform State Laws, August 2–9, 1985.

National Hemlock Society, "Self-Deliverance with Certainty," *Hemlock Quarterly,* No. 30, January 1988.

Nexon, David. "Senator Kennedy's Proposal to Guarantee Basic Health Benefits for All Americans," *Henry Ford Hospital Medical Journal,* Vol. 38, Nos. 2 & 3, 1990, pp. 110–113.

Pepper Commission — U.S. Bipartisan Commission on Comprehensive Health Care.

A Call for Action: Final Report. Washington, DC: Government Printing Office, September 1990a.

Pepper Commission—U.S. Bipartisan Commission on Comprehensive Health Care. *A Call for Action: Supplement to Final Report.* Washington, DC: Government Printing Office, September 1990b.

Prado, C.G. *The Last Choice: Preemptive Suicide in Advanced Age.* Westport, CT: Greenwood Press, 1990.

Pozgar, George. *Legal Aspects of Health Care Administration–4th Edition.* Rockville, MD: Aspen, 1990.

President's Commission for the Study of Ethical Problems in Medicine and Biomedical and Behavioral Research. *Defining Death.* Washington, DC: Government Printing Office, July 1981.

President's Commission for the Study of Ethical Problems in Medicine and Biomedical and Behavioral Research. *Deciding to Forego Life-Sustaining Treatment.* Washington, DC: Government Printing Office, March 1983.

Public Law 93-647. Title XX, Social Services Amendments of 1974, October 1, 1975.

Public Law 97-300. *Job Training Partnership Act.* U.S. Congress, July 1, 1984.

Public Law 100-77. *Stewart B. McKinney Homeless Assistance Act of 1987.* 42 U.S.C. 290, July 22, 1987.

Rabkin, Mitchell T., Gerald Gillerman, and Nancy R. Rice. "Orders Not to Resuscitate," *New England Journal of Medicine,* Vol. 295, 1976, pp. 365–366.

Rakich, Jonathon S., Beaufort B. Longest, and Kurt Darr. *Managing Health Services Organizations.* Philadelphia: W.B. Saunders, 1985.

Raffel, Marshall (ed.). *Comparative Health Systems.* University Park, PA: The Penn State University Press, 1984.

Reuters News Service. "Survey: Don't Prosecute Doctors for Aiding Suicide," Miami, FL: *The Miami Herald,* May 6, 1991, p. 8A.

Rice, Robert. "Change and Continuity in Family Services," *Families in Society: The Journal of Contemporary Human Services,* Vol. 71, No. 1, 1990, pp. 24–31.

Riga, Peter J. *Right to Die or Right to Live?* Gaithersburg, MD: Associated Faculty Press, 1981.

Rigter, Henk. "Euthanasia in the Netherlands: Distinguishing Fact from Fiction", *The Hastings Center Report—Special Supplement,* January/February 1989, pp. 31–32.

Robert Wood Johnson Foundation, "Day Care Center Closes Gap in Services for Disabled Children", *Advances,* Vol. 3, No. 4, Winter 1990, Princeton, NJ, p. 10.

Robins, Philip K. and Samuel Weiner. "An Introduction to the Economic and Policy Issues of Child Care," in *Child Care and Public Policy,* Philip K. Robins and Samuel Weiner, (eds.)., Lexington, MA: Lexington Books, 1978, Chapter 1, pp. 1–15.

Roemer, Milton and Ruth Roemer. *Health Manpower Policies Under Five National Health Care Systems.* U.S.D.H.E.W., Washington, DC: Government Printing Office, 1977.

Roemer, Milton. *Health Care Systems in World Perspective.* Ann Arbor, MI: Health Administration Press, 1976.

Roemer, Milton. *Systems of Health Care.* New York: Springer, 1977.

Saltzman, Amy. *Downshifting: Reinventing Success on a Slower Track.* New York: Harper Collins, 1991.

Satz v. Perlmutter, 362 So. 2d 160 (Fla. Dist. Ct. App. 1978), aff'd 379 So 2d 359 (Fla. Sup. Ct. 1980).

Seitchik, Adam, Jeffrey Zornitsky, and Christopher Edmonds. *Employer Strategies for a Changing Labor Force.* Washington, DC: National Commission for Employment Policy, July 1990.

Senate Bill S.768. *Basic Health Benefits for All Americans Act.* Senate Report 1001-217. U.S. Senate, 101st Congress, 1st Session, Washington, DC: Government Printing Office, November 20, 1989.

Short, P., A. Monheit, and K. Beauregard. *A Profile of Uninsured Americans.* DHHS Pub. No. (PHS) 89-3443. Rockville, MD: NCHSR&HCTA, September 1989.

Skinner, Wickham. "The Impact of Changing Technology on the Working Environment," in *Work in America: The Decade Ahead,* Clark Kerr and Jerome Rosow (eds.)., New York: Van Nostrand Reinhold, 1979, Chapter 11, pp. 204–230.

Sochen, June. *Herstory.* New York: Alfred, 1974.

Society for the Right to Die. *Checklist Chart of Living Will Laws.* New York: Society for the Right to Die, 1985.

State of Washington. *House Initiative 119.* Olympia, WA: Statute Law Committee, Office of the Code Reviser, January 18, 1991.

Steinfels, M. *Who's Minding the Children?: The History and Politics of Day Care in America.* New York: Simon and Schuster, 1973.

Streets, Donald, (ed.). *Administering Day Care and Preschool Programs.* Boston: Allyn and Bacon, 1982.

Stuart, Paul. "A Framework for Cross-National Comparisons of Social Welfare Systems," in *New Horizons of Social Welfare and Policy.* Brij Mohan, (ed.). Cambridge, MA: Schenkman Books, 1985, pp. 77–88.

Terris, Milton. "The Three World Systems of Medical Care: Trends and Prospects," *American Journal of Public Health,* Vol. 68, No. 11, November 1978, pp. 1125–1131.

Thorman, George. *Homeless Families.* Springfield, IL: Charles C Thomas, 1988.

Thorman, George. *Day Care: An Emerging Crisis.* Springfield, IL: Charles C Thomas, 1989.

Toffler, Alvin. *Future Shock.* New York: Random House, 1970.

Toffler, Alvin. *The Third Wave.* New York: Bantam Books, 1980.

Toffler, Alvin. *The Adaptive Corporation.* New York: McGraw-Hill, 1985.

Toffler, Alvin. *Powershift.* New York: Bantam Books, 1990.

U.S. Conference of Mayors. *The Growth of Hunger and Homelessness and Poverty in America's Cities.* Washington, DC: U.S. Conference of Mayors, 1986.

U.S. Conference of Mayors. *A Status Report on Homeless Families in American Cities.* Washington, DC: U.S. Conference of Mayors, 1987.

U.S. Conference of Mayors. *The Continuing Growth of Hunger and Homelessness and Poverty in America's Cities: 1987.* Washington, DC: U.S. Conference of Mayors, December 1987.

U.S. Congress. *Stewart B. Mckinney Homeless Assistance Act—Amendments 1990.* U.S. Congress, Reference 101-583, July 10, 1990.

U.S. Department of Commerce. Bureau of the Census. *Statistical Abstract of the United States—1989—109th Edition.* Washington, DC: Government Printing Office, January 1989.

U.S. Department of Housing and Urban Development. *A Report to the Secretary on the Homeless and Emergency Shelters.* Washington, DC: Office of Policy Development and Research, DHUD, 1984.

U.S. General Accounting Office. *Job Training Partnership Act: Information on Set-Aside Funding for Assistance to Older Workers.* Washington, DC: Government Printing Office, January 1990.

U.S. House of Representatives. *A Discursive Dictionary of Health Care.* Washington, DC: Government Printing Office, February 1976.

U.S. House of Representatives. *Homelessness in America—II.* Washington, DC: Subcommittee on Housing and Community Development, Serial 98-64, January 25, 1984.

U.S. House of Representatives, Select Committee on Aging. *Dying with Dignity.* Publication No. 99-549, Washington, DC: Government Printing Office, October 1, 1985.

U.S. House of Representatives. *Homeless Families: A Neglected Crisis.* Washington, DC: Committee on Government Operations, House Report 99-982, October 9, 1986.

U.S. House of Representatives. Subcommittee on Labor-Management Relations. *Hearings on Economic Dislocation and Worker Adjustment Assistance Act, H.R. 1122, Serial 100-53, March 17, 1987.* Washington, DC: Government Printing Office, 1988.

U.S. House of Representatives. Committee on Education and Labor. *Job Training Partnership Act Amendments of 1990, Report 101-747.* Washington, DC: Government Printing Office, September 24, 1990.

U.S. Senate. Committee on Labor and Human Resources. *The Economic Dislocation and Worker Adjustment Assistance Act—S. 538—Report 100-62.* Washington, DC: Government Printing Office, June 2, 1987.

U.S. Senate. Subcommittee on Employment and Productivity. *Oversight on the Job Training Partnership Act, 1985.* Washington, DC: Government Printing Office, July 1 and 2, and August 7, 1985.

U.S. Senate. Committee on Labor and Human Resources. *Education and Training Partnership Act—Hearings Before the Subcommittee on Employment and Productivity on S. 1990.* Washington, DC: Government Printing Office, February 19 and 25, 1986.

Waldman, Saul. *National Health Insurance Proposals.* DHEW Pub. No. (SSA 76-11920), Washington, DC: Government Printing Office, February, 1976.

Walton, Richard E. "Innovative Restructuring of Work," in *The Worker and the Job: Coping with Change,* Jerome M. Rosow (ed.)., Englewood Cliffs, NJ: Prentice-Hall, 1974, Chapter 6, pp. 145–176.

Weber, Gerald I. "National Health Insurance: Issues in Conflict," in *Politics of Health,* Douglass Cater and Philip Lee, (eds.). New York: MEDCOM Press, 1972, Chapter 6, pp. 98–114.

Weissburg, Carl and Jay N. Hartz. "The Issue of Feeding: It is the Most Troubling of

Life Support Questions," *Federation of American Hospitals Review,* November/December 1983, pp. 42–43.

Whitebook, M. et al., "Who's Minding the Child Care Workers?" *Children Today,* January 1981, pp. 2–6.

Zagoria, Sam. "Policy Implications and Future Agendas," in *The Worker and the Job: Coping with Change,* Jerome M. Rosow (ed.)., Englewood Cliffs, NJ: Prentice-Hall, 1974, Chapter 7, pp. 177–201.

Zigler, E.F. and E.W. Gordon, (eds.). *Day Care: Scientific and Social Policy Issues.* Boston: Auburn, 1982.

AUTHOR INDEX

145

Heller, W., 117
Helton, A., 47
Hollingshead, A., 61
Holloway, S., 31, 63
Hopps, J., 102
Houle, C., 86
Humphry, D., 129
Hunter, A., 51
Hutchison, E., 109
Huttman, E., 62, 66–67, 123
Hyman, H., 6, 7

J

Jackson, J., 50
Jansson, B., 10
Jimenez, M., 4, 9, 11–14
Johnson, H., 12
Jones, M., 60, 69, 77–78
Joy, R., 5

K

Kahn, A., 114–115
Kahn, E., 3, 43, 78
Karger, H., 31–32, 115
Kamerman, S., 114–115
Katz, L., 114
Keeling, R., 44
Kennedy, E., 114
Klarman, H., 61
Kleiman, C., 84
Kohlert, N., 4, 31
Kubler-Ross, E., 38

L

Lamm, R., 127
Landesman, H., 60
Landesman, T., 22
Larson, M., 110, 112, 114, 118
Lebeaux, C., 5
Lee, P., 4, 11
Leiby, J., 14
Leutz, W., 17
Le Vee, W., 44
Lewis, B., 46
Lewis, F., 78
Lewis, H., 19

Lewis, O., 33
Light, D., 19
Loudon, D., 63
Luce, B., 5

M

Macarov, D., 19, 30, 120, 122–126
MacStravic, R., 63
Mailick, M., 66
Maloney, C., 60
Marieskind, H., 50
Marmor, T., 9
Marsden, D., 121
Martin, D., 44, 48
Martin, G., 13, 113
Marver, J., 110, 112, 114, 118
Masi, D., 21
Maslow, A., 35, 62
Maynard, F., 113
McCool, B., 19
McGarrahan, E., 116–117
McKillip, J., 67, 69
McLeer, S., 47
McNearney, W., 34
McNeely, R., 46
Meddin, B., 67
Meriam, L., 99
Miller, I., 121
Minahan, A., 3, 13, 18, 62, 78
Miringoff, M., 6, 9, 85
Mishkin, B., 127
Mitchell, A., 61
Momeni, J., 109
Monheit, A., 96–98
Morris, R., 4, 9
Moss, M., 100
Mott, V., 60
Mowbray, A., 5
Moyerman, S., 95, 100
Mullan, F., 4, 5
Mumford, L., 34
Murphy, M., 64, 72–76
Murray, C., 31

N

Nader, R., 60
Naisbitt, J., 30

SUBJECT INDEX